Inner and Outer Landscapes

About the Author

Selma Lea Bach grew up close to nature, and since the beginning of her life, she has considered nature to be her greatest teacher. Her writing unveils the unity between the human being and the natural world. She has travelled widely and dwelled in remote parts of the globe where secrets of life and nature were passed on to her through the wisdom of natives and the landscapes surrounding them. Her hope as an author is to open the reader's awareness to what a miracle life truly is and to help them in beginning to find the source of their own existence.

Selma Lea Bach

Inner and Outer Landscapes

Olympia Publishers
London

www.olympiapublishers.com
OLYMPIA PAPERBACK EDITION

Copyright © Selma Lea Bach 2024

The right of Selma Lea Bach to be identified as author of
this work has been asserted in accordance with sections 77 and 78 of
the Copyright, Designs and Patents Act 1988.

All Rights Reserved

No reproduction, copy or transmission of this publication
may be made without written permission.
No paragraph of this publication may be reproduced,
copied or transmitted save with the written permission of the publisher,
or in accordance with the provisions
of the Copyright Act 1956 (as amended).

Any person who commits any unauthorised act in relation to
this publication may be liable to criminal
prosecution and civil claims for damage.

A CIP catalogue record for this title is
available from the British Library.

ISBN: 978-1-80074-574-2

This is a work of fiction.
Names, characters, places and incidents originate from the writer's
imagination. Any resemblance to actual persons, living or dead, is
purely coincidental.

First Published in 2024

Olympia Publishers
Tallis House
2 Tallis Street
London
EC4Y 0AB
Printed in Great Britain

Acknowledgements

Thank you to all the people I met on my path who helped me shape this story, and a special thanks to my editor Jim Powell for his attentive care on every single sentence of my work.

A woman's journey to search for her roots and place of belonging on this Earth and to the sky above.

"*Your children are not your children.*
They are sons and daughters of Life's longing for itself.
They come through you but not from you.
And though they are with you yet they belong not to you.

You may give them your love but not your thoughts,
For they have their own thoughts.
You may house their bodies but not their souls,
For their souls dwell in the house of tomorrow, which you cannot visit, not even in your dreams.
You may strive to be like them, but seek not to make them like you.
For life goes not backward nor tarries with yesterday.
You are the bows from which your children as living arrows are sent forth.
The archer sees the make upon the path of the infinite, and He bends you with His might that His arrows may go swift and far.
Let your bending in the archer's hand be for gladness.
For even as He loves the arrow that flies,
so He also loves the bow that is stable."

— Kahlil Gibran

Before you begin reading, please take note: this is fiction, a story written in the name of a child I carried in my womb but chose not to bring into this world. This book was a way for me to live out the life she might have lived and to heal from the pain of following my decision. The stories of the people in the book are mostly stories from my own life, as told through the voice of my daughter as I imagine her. They are all true. They came from those encountered on my path and from landscapes I have seen with my own eyes.

I am not aiming to be politically correct in any way. I try only to give words to the events I experienced and the stories I heard on my travels.

This book is entirely dedicated to my daughter and to her father, whom I loved deeply. It is a story of all the challenges one must face on one´s path to know oneself, as well as a celebration of Mother Earth, of She who gives birth to all life. May my daughter rest peacefully while I give birth to the story she never got the opportunity to tell.

- Selma Lea Bach

Chapter 1
The Sacredness of Pregnancy

I was five years old when I heard the first peep ever about my real father. His name was Ammar. A mere fledgling, I was too young to really understand what this sudden knowledge of my origins might mean. I reacted by rejecting my mother for a few days and solemnly pecking at my food. The emotional shock wave soon resolved itself, but I was old enough to start wondering and questioning introspectively. In a few days I emerged from my tangled nest of thoughts and squawked an indelicate disquietude into the air: "Are you, then, my real mother?"

She immediately reassured me she had carried me in her own womb and that I was the greatest miracle of her existence: a true manifestation of life itself. When she became pregnant with me, for the first time she understood the miracle of life, and how she would understand and accept that miracle of life outside before she had felt it growing inside of her.

When only a few weeks old in her womb, I told her my name. One day when she was sitting on a bench, taking in the colors of a setting Sun, she cupped her hands around her belly, and the name Alanna emerged instantly. From that day on, she began to feel my entire spirit within and everywhere surrounding her.

Later on, in life, she whispered into my ear, "there is nothing more sacred than being pregnant."

It humbled her to feel that extraordinary ability we have to bring something out of seeming nothingness, whether the creation was myself, my name, or a revelation of my origin. Each new arrival seemed an extension of herself, yet so vastly different and so individual. An expression of life itself and the very fruits of a unity between a man and a woman. I at least had been the result of a deep love my mother shared with a man from the Arab world I had just learned about myself. My mother often told me she had really loved my father, but that certain things had rendered her unable to stay with him.

For one, he was considerably older than her, at least twice her age, although his soul remained young and fresh. The scars and wrinkles on his body were proof of a life lived full of challenges and gained wisdom.

After that day of revelation, she began telling me stories about my father. Of his adventures, of the places he lived, and of the culture from which he had emerged. Every night I would ask for a new tale and she would tell me one after the other. I loved hearing each, even though as I grew older, I found it difficult to believe all the stories were actually real. Nevertheless, as I journeyed from one year to the next, they formed a fountain of inspiration within my inner world. Like moving shadows, their mysterious landscapes shaped my imagination so deeply that much later in life they would return and take me by the hand, and transport me away into a most extraordinary journey of self-discovery to the very roots of my existence and into the heart of life itself.

As if she had been feeding on and living from those stories herself, my mother always shared them with me. Later on, I came to learn that perhaps all these tales helped her compensate for all the adventures she had not managed to live.

Even when I was still quite young, she often spoke to me as if I were an adult, as if she felt compelled to share her understanding of this life with me before the outside world and society would entirely shape me with a different one. Later on in life, I came to love her for having done that. Her nourishing care enticed me from the beginning, when I was still in her belly and she started whispering secrets and telling me stories about beauty and goodness. While still pregnant, she would often take me out into nature to familiarize me with certain landscapes so that I would gain a prenatal sense of them before my arrival. She would introduce me to the winds: the soft breezes barely caressing your cheek. And later, when I was a little older, she opened my awareness to storm winds, so wild and powerful they could take down entire buildings, convulse an ocean into a laboring abyss, demolish entire worlds. She believed that the wind was the spirit of this world. Without it, there would be no exchange of anything. She taught me to stop and listen to the stories the wind carries on its endless roams around this globe. Full of secrets of overheard conversation from people and encounters with lonely landscapes, it somehow knows all things, and connects all corners of the world with each other. Warm winds from the deserts gushing with soft memories of ever-shifting waves of dunes rising and falling under the eye of a godly Sun. Freezing blasts from the forests of Siberia reminding us of the necessary endurance needed to survive those frozen worlds. Yet the languages of the wind, the mother tongues of those regions, speak only to those who really know how to listen, to let go of themselves for a while.

    My mother always showed me how each outer landscape mirrors a corresponding interior inner landscape. She taught me that the outer one reflects and transports us to our inner soul landscapes. She showed me how the two landscapes illumine one another, how we are all citizens of these two worlds at the same time — one inner, one outer — and how it can sometimes be difficult for us to combine and unify them. That difficulty arises especially in these times when materialism has us hypnotized so deeply that the inner hardly retains its place, its value, its very existence.

"Every period of history presents its challenges", my mother would tell me. These times, she felt, surely, we are removed so far from the laws of nature that we would soon end up depleting this world's life resources entirely and having exchanged every natural process with a machine. She thought that if we were not careful, we would all end up like robots in a virtual game.

As I grew, I often found that she had been a little too extreme and pessimistic in her judgements about where evolution was going. I found this world to be still rich and abundant in nature, with places to explore and connect to the source we all come from. But maybe the hardship of her own life left her with a feeling of defeat and despair.

Bringing me into this life had almost cost the price of her own life. She was, according to herself, born into this life with a weak constitution, with frail health. She always told the same story about a genetically marred liver function she had sadly inherited from her own father's side of the family. From her mother's side arrived the genetics that must have descended from the strongest warriors, the Vikings, because I never saw my grandmother suffer ill health. She was the halest woman I ever knew, so brimming with vitality that I would deeply question whether age means anything else other than a random number.

I don't think anyone was ever able to find out what was really wrong with my mother's body, considering that her father lived till he was almost ninety, remaining healthy enough to take care of himself throughout. I thought it could have not been that bad, but the reality was that my mother had always suffered pain, pain that made her life almost impossible to bear. When she became pregnant with me, she knew that having me could ruin her ability to heal from her own pain and bring about change in this world. So, she deeply considered letting go of me and sending me back to whence I had come. At the last minute, though, just before she was scheduled to have an abortion, she chose to keep me anyway, despite the opinions of others about this being too heavy a burden for her to carry. She would always justify her decision with the paradox that by giving herself away, she became herself.

Even though she managed the pregnancy better than anyone expected, including herself, by the time I arrived she was so weak that she could hardly take care of me or herself. She passed on all her nutrients and life forces to me, and it left her in a bit of a hopeless state. I arrived healthy and instantly found myself in harmony with my new surroundings here on Earth. Of course, this part is something I do not remember, but something I have been told often by those who witnessed my first stage of life.

Due to the circumstances surrounding my mother's health, I grew up partly with my grandmother and my aunty, my mother's sister, two people who have been almost as important to me in my first years as my own mother. When I revisit memories of those times, I feel an ocean of love surrounding me, a peaceful pace of life with plenty of time and space for playing and discovering this world.

Sometimes when my mother was tired, my grandmother would come and take me to her home in the countryside for a few days. There she would show me her garden, so I could crawl around amongst beautiful flowers and touch the Earth with my tiny feet. Then she would cook and feed me the healthiest and most natural meals this world has ever known. She took me to swim in wild forest lakes. She made me laugh when she splashed cold water gently on my face. Through her love and patience, she taught me this Earth is a wonderful and safe place to live. I never felt scared to go to sleep when closing my eyes after a day fully lived. My inner vision was full of images of flowers, lakes, and the warm and illuming love of my family.

As I grew a little older, I slowly learned this world is not only roses and light, but that the path is often also full of weeds and chisels, challenges resulting in both victories and defeats. I learned that all light also leaves shadow. I grew into a feeling that life was surely both better and worse than I could have ever hoped for. Far more extraordinary and larger than what it had seemed like at one stage, life's path became equally difficult and simple, beautiful and painful, just as light and darkness know themselves only through each other.

Chapter 2
Nature Is the Greatest Architect of All

I grew up in a small autonomic area in the outskirts of my city. A little treasure hidden in the heart of Denmark. A place where people such as my mother found a pocket of escape from the bureaucratic society dominant in those times. We were a part of what was a village of around two hundred small wooden houses. People from all walks of life were living there, some starkly alternative, some holding important positions in the system, whereas some, such as my mother, just wanted to grow a little garden and live her days in peace from the stress and rush of society. It was actually illegal to live there all year around because the property belonged to the government and was rented to us for almost nothing. "But sometimes, it is better to live with a risk than to risk not living at all," my mother would always say.

The location of my village was just on the outskirts of the city, an extension of the suburbs, escaping straight into the arms of mother nature. A huge lake right outside our door was home to thousands of birds and insects. Cows grazed on the banks of the lake, and everything was left to grow wild and abundantly, just as nature intended. My mother would always tell me that nature was the greatest architect of all, and I felt proud to be living within the arms of her creations and not among the concrete and artificial lights of cities. I was always told that no light is more powerful than the Sun, who can light up this entire Earth and bring everything alive. No streetlight is as good for navigating as the stars lighting up the sky.

Once upon a time, navigators found their directions on long journeys by consulting the heavens. And there is even a famous pilgrim route reaching all the way through Spain, Camino de Santiago. It follows the Milky Way from the beginning all the way to the very end of the country, which is a place once believed to be the end of the world. My mother, when young, had once walked the entire length of that route. She was hoping to find herself on the way, or even better, find God Himself. Some say that when you look for yourself, you'll find God, and when you look for God, you'll find yourself. Surely there is some truth to that, but I'm not sure my mother felt that she had found either. She loved feeling the enrapturing landscapes unfold with each step, learning that we are all pilgrims upon this Earth.

"If God gave us feet, it must be so we can walk our own way home," she would say. "It is amazing to move through this world at the pace of your own footsteps taking you from one part of this world to another, through open and dusty roads to high mountain peaks, and then one day after weeks and weeks of walking to arrive at the coast, to wash your sore body and feet in the cold salty water and sink into the boundless relief of having reached your destination." Soon she discovered that the relief of having finally reached her goal also came with an emptiness. She realized it is surely the journey itself that is the destination, not the other way around.

Sometimes the journey can feel endless. In life, when you reach the mountaintop you were aiming for, your vision becomes wider and you can see all the peaks you have yet to climb.

As for knowledge and wisdom: one answered question often leads to a sequence of more, which can continue in what seems an infinite path of knowing.

I could tell you many more beautiful stories from my childhood. The only thing missing from them, though, was the presence of my father. The bedtime stories my mother used to share so openly with me became less and less as I grew older, maybe as a result of her memory about them slowly fading as the years went by. When I asked what had happened to my father, she could not give me an answer. Only that he had left civilization and was probably living in the desert somewhere away from all contact with people and places, except for a few local people and some animals. She could not know if he was still there or if he long ago had crossed the bridge to the unknown and left his body behind.

"Did he know I exist?" I once asked when I was old enough to know to ask such a question. And so that day, she told me he had disappeared entirely from this Earth before she had time even to know she was carrying me in her belly. She told me he was a man of extremes. As for the people of his culture, they gave him his all-or-nothing attitude. So, when my mother told him she wanted to take a few steps alone in life and stand on her own two feet, he reacted strongly and instantly concluded that without her his life was not worth much any more. Being tired from living, all he wanted was to live in peace with Mother Nature. And since that day, my mother has never heard a word from him. She tried a few times to contact some family members, but all they ever told her was that he no longer wished to have any contact with her. He was a man of knowledge who had spent his entire life studying and learning to do and build anything on his own.

"You could have asked your father anything, and he would have known the answer," my mother told tell me. He was a man of truth, always seeking the highest form of understanding, and always confronting himself as well as others with his high morality and deepest values in life. These included qualities of beauty and goodness, but sometimes they would also lead him down a blind road of constant judgement of himself and others. That resulted in his relationships always ending in conflict, so that mostly he had to walk alone. Nobody could ever live up to his high sense of morality. He was different than anyone else you would ever meet, my mother would tell me. He was one of a kind, struggling on his path to freedom and to know the truth about life, not wasting much time on anything other than trying to perfect himself and gain more knowledge about this world.

He was born in Syria, in the city Damascus. His family roots had descended from the prophet Muhammad. His father made himself the richest man in all of Syria. As a young man his father travelled to Ghana, where he started a tailoring shop. It became so successful that within a few years another twenty shops opened up in his name around Accra, the capital. As a result of his father's success, my own father grew up with furniture covered in gold, a house filled with wealthy belongings, and a dining table always set with the most delicious and expensive food.

When he was only a few years old, a civil war broke out in Syria and his whole family had to flee to Lebanon. There he spent his youth in Beirut, a place of civilization and knowledge often referred to as the Paris of the Middle East. The beauty of the architecture and the knowledge of the people had helped form him, but as everything else in this world, those times were also to come to an end. Syrians were never really welcome in Lebanon. They were the poorest people in the Middle East. The Lebanese did not respect them. So, when a new civil war broke out, he and his family once again fled to find safety in another land. Having lost almost all their fortune during times of unrest, they ended up escaping to Egypt and living an almost average life in Cairo.

The two years my mother spent with him were truly magical, almost not of this world, as she would say. Ammar showed her worlds and values of great beauty. He made her understand herself in the eyes of the universe, made her feel like the most perfect woman this world had ever known. He offered all his love right at her feet. She loved him more than anyone else for those years and they shared the most sacred unity two people can possibly feel with one another. They shared a deep understanding of each other's beings and a common reality and view on life. Both knew that all in this world is interconnected with nature and all living things.

As time passed, however, Ammar wanted more and more from her. He wanted her to become half of himself, to make a promise of eternal unity, and to never be apart from him for even one second of his life. These needs were more than my mother was ready for at the time. The truths he had found in life were so strongly engrained within him that he would not accept any other understandings. So as time passed, my mother found herself unable to find her own truth, to live within her own understanding. As a consequence, her body grew weaker. Her spirit started withering. She felt she was losing herself in him. And by the end, despite the fact that she still loved him deeply, she felt she had no other choice than to leave him.

She left. And with her, deep within herself, she discovered she was carrying the greatest gift of her life, as she always put it: me.

"I wish you could have known your father because you are a

lot like him," she would often tell me. I'm quite different in both looks and nature from my mother. Her body was slender, and she was not tall. She had a friendly, slightly rounded face and wide cheekbones. She looked healthy even though the years of life were starting to show and the struggles of her body had left certain marks of pain in her expressions. Her smile, especially, often revealed that she had to struggle to maintain it, even though she generally felt life was fully worth smiling at most of the time. Sometimes when I watched her cooking, I could almost imagine how she would look when she grew elderly, her white hair like her own mother's, wrinkles around her eyes from smiling, and deep lines haunting her forehead like the paths of the Milky Way.

My hair was brown, my skin darker, absorbing the power of the heavenly body of the Sun, as if my genes carried the memories of life after life, lived under the relentless, redemptive Sun of my forefathers. And now, only by a few rays of that golden orb, my genes are reminded of their entire history. I am taller than my mother, my body a little more robust, more solid than hers. My eyes are an earthy brown rather than spacious blue. My features surely reveal an abundance of strength. All through my school years, at least among the girls, my body has been strong, fit, and always ready for what I wanted it to do. I often feel my whole being resides within it: my spirit and soul just as much as my head and hands. I never really understood what my mother meant when she constantly separated body and soul when trying to make sense of whatever separation she had always felt in hers. But further down the road, I began to understand there must be some truth to her understanding. If spirit does not transcend body, how would anything survive on the other side of death? This body belongs only to this world as a member of this earthly kingdom. Everything here returns to whence it came. But the soul and spirit body go elsewhere. At least this is how I imagine it. But of course, I have no proof of such things even being true, and I can only wait for my own death one day to come along to confirm those beliefs, or not.

Growing up, I would not say that I suffered from the absence of my father. I mean, I did not know any other reality. There were a few different men in my mother's life back then. One was there for the first many years of my life. He had taken on the role of a father and had given me all the love a little new one could have ever wished for. He was not my real father, though, so that relationship ended, not because they had stopped loving each other, but certain circumstances made it difficult to continue. Possibly it was because of my mother's poor health. People tended to support and understand for a while, but when things did not change over time, they became tired and exhausted. Then both partners realized they would feel better and freer without each other. Already, then, I started questioning why it was so difficult for most people to keep that flame burning, to not start taking each other for granted, to not fall in to the patterns of familiarity and comfort. Is love only circumstantial, or does it spring from some eternal value? These are the questions I would ask myself. Of course, these are questions that could take a lifetime to answer. I could only hope I would one day live my way into the answers.

A few more men came in and out of our lives, but none managed to endure the challenge of time and commitment. She loved them all, and they her. Because they loved her, they also loved me, for I remained the most important creature in her life.

Chapter 3
The Mystery of Life

My grandfather also exerted a strong influence on my upbringing. He was a sensitive and wise man. Though life had been a little too hard on this delicate being, he managed to keep something utterly sublime alive within himself. When I was a little girl, he would often take me into the garden, where he grew food and medicine for the entire community. I shall never forget the smell of soil just turned and prepared to become a host for new life. He would never allow me to just look on passively. Instead, he invited me to help by placing tiny seeds in a row, with the same distance between each, giving them a little water, and covering them carefully again with soil. He told me that the personal engagement in that process awakens some relation to the plants later on. First, I could not understand how a seed could possibly turn out to become something—a carrot or cucumber. How was it even possible? I felt puzzled by the mystery of life. Looking at the dark brown soil, I could not find any of the colors or shapes that would one day make up what I knew a carrot to look like. My grandfather would explain to me how the whole of this universe comes together to create these shapes and colors and how important a role each planet and star plays in the becoming of these plants. All of the cosmos can be found within each seed, and all forms of life depend on all other forms of life since nothing in this universe is separate, existing without the other. One day he cut a beetroot in two, revealing concentric, patterned lines and circles.

"You see? This is the planetary movement of Juniper around Earth," he would point out, my eyes tracing a perfect circle in the structure of the vegetable.

"We know how much the moon's orbit controls all water on Earth, pulls it toward us and let's go of it again, over and over. So why would the other planets not also affect our lives?" He prophesied that one day this would all become common knowledge for all humans, but would take a while and require a complete shift in the understanding of life for modern science to come to such discoveries.

Because we live in a time of separation, most believe the universe emerged as a complete accident, a sequence of coincidences, random events eventually leading to the becoming of this extraordinary planet we call home. My grandfather surely did not accept such a reductive understanding of life. He saw and felt otherwise internally. He lacked the power, however, to truly come out and show the world around him what he saw and knew within himself as reality. Yet he managed to give me a feeling of how life is much larger than one could ever imagine, more interconnected, wiser, and far more intelligent than any computer or modern device.

No matter how diligently I absorbed my grandfather's lessons, at school I was not the best student. I often suffered from complete indifference to and impatience with classroom topics. I spent entire days daydreaming and looking out the window, imagining who I would become when I grew older and what adventures life had planned for me. I did not find school capable of satisfying my deepest inner longings. I often felt a little empty inside because the knowledge presented seemed dry, separate, and meaningless. As I grew older, I began feeling suspicious about the ability of compartmentalized knowledge to convey all of what reality truly involves. The seeds my family had planted in me from early on had begun to sprout. I could no longer accept the same vision of reality as the one presented by the educational system. Perhaps we all somehow fall victim to our own awareness. Our understanding of this reality constantly comes down to what we have been told life is, unless we have a strong inner feeling that teaches us elsehow. And because the girls in my class were interested mainly in boys and gossip, while the boys remained interested mainly in sports and computer games, I understood that neither had ever been initiated into an understanding where life is far greater than that.

In the end, our perceptions of this world mostly come down to the stories we have been told about life. To change that reality, we must tell new and different stories about who we are and where we come from. This requires asking different questions. Sometimes this can come about when something difficult has happened in our lives: an illness, a car accident, the death of a close family member. And such tragedies can initiate some deeper realization of what is real.

For example, losing someone to death makes one think about where that person went. Did they just disappear into the dark cold soil of a graveyard, or did they travel elsewhere and continue living in some other distant realm of planets, galaxies, solar systems? Will they ever return here to Earth in a new body, born into a different country, born into a different sex than before, unable to remember anything of their previous lives here, accepting their new reality as if it were the only life they have ever known? The questions might be endless but might often lead to more questions reaching increasingly further outward, just like the cosmos itself.

I remember the day I realized that nobody really knew anything about these things. It was a shock to discover because I imagine most children rely on their parents for answers to such questions. My mother had always talked to me about death as something natural, as an extension of life, as a bridge to cross or a new beginning right at the end of a long journey.

"Life knows itself only in the eyes of death," my mother would tell me. It is something we all know will come one day. As a matter of fact, death is the only thing we can know for sure about our lives. Even though she knew exactly what would happen, where she would go, how it would feel, who she would meet, and how it would all look, I was not as convinced as her. I even think she was often looking forward for her time to come, longing for the liberation of body she was sure she would receive to return back to the spirit realms from whence she had descended. I always felt a little suspicious about her being so strongly convinced about these things. Maybe she had read too many New Age spiritual books and slowly just accepted these descriptions as a complete reality. At least I promised myself to find out on my own. Many seek answers in religion, in science, and in spirituality, but I simply prefer to walk with my feet bare, feel the wind in my hair, the rain on my skin, the Sun on my face, and then the rest does not really matter. Why should I spend so much time imagining worlds elsewhere, when this one is so magical and alive? Why would I risk missing the wonder of this one? No, that could not happen to me. I preferred to walk my own path, wherever it would take me, and accept only what I could really prove or know to be real.

From the outside, my teenage years were mostly like those of most, with no exceptions from the awkwardness of that age, the insecurities of identity and the self-absorption of believing you are the very axis of this universe and everything is created only for you. I went through it all: parties, alcohol, boys, a bit of drugs, and a phase where I thought painting my whole face with makeup actually made me more beautiful. Luckily, later, the mirror told me otherwise. Those years went by fast, maybe because I wanted them to. I found them a little too messy for my real inner world, that something of magic I used to feel about life had been taken away. I realized that looking for magic through psychedelics or in the company of others was a quixotic quest. I found growing older to be the best medicine and bridge out of that void.

I had always felt a little foreign among the company of others. To find a place of rest and belonging, I went to nature. Her company became for my soul what food is for the body. I needed her beauty and wisdom to feel whole and at home. She taught me about my true nature by showing me her own. The more time I spent alone with her, the more I started to see and hear. Sometimes I could almost pick up on conversations between old trees in the forests and green mosses, their communications about weather or drifting continents. These were communicated at such a different pace than any language spoken in the modern world that I felt drawn to become quieter and to listen more carefully inside.

This is how, without even knowing, I learned to meditate. Nature filled me with feelings of peace and calmness. It helped me arrange my thoughts and remain in balance through times of inner and outer tumult. I would go as far as to say that nature saved my life several times. When I found this world to be a cruel and difficult place to be in, she was always there with her beauty and stability. She taught me through the moon that it is okay to go through phases and by the Sun to always rise again despite the clouds and the rain. From nature, I learned most of what I know today.

Chapter 4
Every Day Is a New Birth

The earth had taken several tours around the sun before I one day found myself at the age of twenty-one in earthly counting. My birthday had not been anything to really talk about because my mother had an opinion that every day is a new birth and every night another death. She never made a big deal out of a birthday, even though upon the dawning of my twenty-first year she wrote me a beautiful, long letter. It told me how proud she was to be my mother and how this very day twenty-one years ago had been the very best day of her entire life. We had never had much money, so presents were always simple. Often, I would receive a new fruit tree for the garden, one that I could see grow every year, and eventually eat and enjoy the fruit.

After reading the letter, I went to throw away the envelope, when I realized it was not empty. Out fell a piece of jewelry. It landed on the floor right in front of me. I picked it up and looked at it carefully. It was a beautiful, thin, and delicate pendant of silver metal with an engraved star in the middle. It looked to be quite an old antique. The design was a bit rustic, but I instantly liked it and placed it around my neck. Later that day my mother told me it was a piece of jewelry she had received on a birthday, from my father. Ammar bought it for her from a local jewelry maker in the desert somewhere, and the symbolism of the star in the middle of the circle was an old Amazigh symbol of peace. Because my mother's name is Selma (Salma in Arabic meaning peace, or the peaceful one), my father found it perfect for her. I asked her why I had never seen her wearing the pendant, and she told me it reminded her too much of him and those times of her life. It was simply too painful for her to be reminded of all these memories. She needed to move on with her life. Now she felt, though, it was time to pass it on to me. She bought me a new silver chain for it because the original one had not lasted the challenge of time and boredom in an old jewelry box where she had kept it for so many years. Not that I really believed jewelry possessed self-awareness enough to know it was not being used. But still, I believed everything in this world wants to live out its fullest purpose. A piece of beautiful jewelry wants to be worn, a flower to blossom, a tree to bear fruit, an instrument to be strummed, and a human being to love and be loved. I believed that in general, everything in the universe is constantly fighting and struggling to become and bring out its own fullest self.

I really loved the pendant. I instantly put it around my neck and felt a little more like a woman than usual. I had been thinking a lot about turning twenty-one. I was surely not a child any more, and my teenage years had also somehow gone by without me doing anything other than showing up for the ordinary challenges of normal life. Then one day I woke up and realized I was not a child any more. Yet I did not feel I was a woman. It felt as if I had gone away on a long sea journey, leaving behind the coasts of today and yesterday, while the far shores of tomorrow land had not yet arrived. I had been feeling a little wobbly inside for a while, not really finding any solid ground to stand on in this transition, like a sailor on a wave-tossed, unknown sea, but I remembered a line from a Leonard Cohen song: "If you don't become the ocean yourself, you'll always be seasick." Those lines gave me the resilience to stand steady among the waves of change.

When we look to nature, we find that she also is always in constant change, moving from one season to another, flowers blossoming only to wither again, and all within such a dignifying stillness and beauty. Nature asks for nothing, and often she keeps her dreams and memories to herself. Like anyone who gardens or grows things and pays attention, I began to notice nature starting to have suffered enough of human neglect and abuse. More and more, our actions had started to manifest as natural disasters: earthquakes, tsunamis, heavy rains, and forest fires. Over and over, she began screaming now, and I often began wondering when we would really stop, and start to listen.

It is as if the resources of this Earth were a bank account we have just been emptying and emptying, only one day to wake up and realize that the account was empty long ago and that now we are in huge debt to Earth.

"Would it be too late then?" I often asked myself.

Luckily, I also noticed that more and more, we have realized what we do to nature, we do to ourselves. We are not separate from her. We come from her. She does not belong to us, but we to her. And our entire existence depends upon her own. The more we deplete her, the poorer we become, and the more we pollute her, the sicker we become. The result is easy to calculate. One does not need to be a mathematician to understand

I noticed that even in cities, where many have almost forgotten her existence, nature insists on life by showing it in the most unlikely places: sprouting up through cracks in hard concrete or on busily trafficked roads, trying to make this world a little greener. Even on rooftops, she tries to grow some mosses or fungus if humidity allows. I began noticing that everywhere, she is alive and trying to communicate with us, her children.

Often, in areas soiled with pollution, she grows plants that absorb toxins and transform them into life, leaving the Earth healthier and cleaner. She has a way of always healing and restoring herself. The same is true of our bodies if we give them the right conditions and environment.

At that time of my life, I had worked to save money for a while, holding down several jobs in cafes and restaurants, as a house maid in a hotel, along with delivering newspapers in my area in the afternoons. Once I worked as a dishwasher in a fancy hotel chain, but the staff treated me so badly that I ended up breaking a plate in front of my boss and telling him I would never put my feet there again. I left with my back straight, but started to cry as soon as I stepped outside the building. Luckily, I do not think anybody saw that. Only shortly after, I felt proud of my reaction: my strong inner resolve to have stood up for myself like that, and in doing so to have stood up for all the dishwashers coming to work there after me. Because when you free yourself, you also free the world. Like waves in water, freedom ripples outward in rings. One freedom follows another as part of the same ocean of life. The waves of one's own consciousness ripple through the luminous consciousness of the whole universe, and every act, regardless of how small and insignificant, reconfigures the sands lining the shores of the totality of life. Our prisons are also the ones of the world, for whatever happens in the world is only a reflection of our human awareness.

    I wiped those tears from my face and felt better inside than ever before, as if I, in that very moment, for the first time, felt my own oceanic power. That night before going to bed, I said thank you to that terrible hotel owner for having been such an idiot to me. His doings had led me to know myself more deeply, and in that moment, I understood how we need resistance for growth. In the process of fighting for our own lives, we are rewarded with the freedom of doing things we thought were beyond our capacity. I realized that sometimes the worst can also be the best. That night my last thought had been of the future, of what challenges it might bring, and where those challenges would eventually lead me. I felt excited for the path ahead.

Because my mother always insisted on making a career as a writer, money was always scarce. It was not that she was really even that good of a writer or had worked at it for her entire life, but one morning she woke up and suddenly felt that writing was exactly what she always wanted to do. Considering her health, it was also the perfect profession for her. She could stay home tending the garden, cooking, playing music, and still reaching out to the world. Her writing skills came as a second thought. I don't think she really even knew the rules of grammar. She had never attended much school when she was young. She insisted that writing be her all. She remembered feeling what Mark Twain once felt, that "the two most important days in your life is the day you are born and the day you know why."

For my mother, that why was her love of writing. Writing provided her with the perfect bridge between her inner world and her outer, from the visible to more invisible realms. Through writing, she felt she gained a voice strong enough to at least try to bring it out. Writing changed her, saved her life several times from the void of reality, and led her onto paths of discovery and creativity. She could not imagine herself doing anything else. Despite the meager living she scratched out, she insisted on continuing, and never compromised by taking an ordinary job somewhere. She always said that by doing so, she would have paid the price of her own soul.

I always both loved and hated her extreme opinions. At times it felt difficult for me to find my own truth. After all, I had been infused with the spirit of her stories since the very first day of my life. Because of her persistence, she also managed to write a few novels. They had been published by some New Age book publisher, sold quite well in the beginning, but soon were forgotten and left to collect dust on some hidden shelves somewhere, her few fans dribbling away in pursuit of other interests.

Sometimes a spiritual magazine or a publisher passionate about climate change would ask her to write a paper on a certain topic. She loved to give her fullest to such projects and enjoyed every minute. Sadly, quite often they would end up editing it a lot, taking out certain parts because they found her opinions to be too radical and disturbing for their readers.

"Nobody really likes to hear the truth," she would tell me, "and the ones who tell it often become unpopular."

That is how it has been all throughout history. For instance, the first person to understand that we are carriers of bacteria, Antonie Philips van Leeuwenhoek, in the 1670s, became the brunt of his medical colleagues' jokes. He even ended up losing his job and only many years later did the world discover he had been right all the while.

We like the world as it is. Or as we think it is. New ideas and understandings can bring out our fear of the unknown, and a new discovery can truly be perceived as a threat to those holding certain established opinions about reality.

Because all my mother's efforts as a writer resulted in some success but never a stable income, my grandmother would often help us out a little. She had inherited a little sum from her father before he left this world, and sometimes she would come and fill up our house with healthy and tasty food, leaving a little money on the table and never asking for anything in return. My grandmother was an exceedingly generous woman. I think she felt happiest when she was able to give and to share what she had with others. And we appreciated my grandmother's help, because even the men who came in and out of my mother's life were not able to provide much. They had all been artists, musicians, or spiritual teachers, and these kinds of professions often do not shower down earthly wealth: only visions and ideals. Those who have the capacity to think and act differently are often the ones who have no position in society to make changes in a world mostly driven my money and eternal economic growth. So, sadly, none of them managed to effect any measurable change. Despite their many attempts to change this world, they have mostly, like my mother, made peace with a quiet life close to nature, away from the fast-moving world of modern civilization.

I have shared with you many things about my life up till now because I believe them to be important as you follow me on my journey further into this story and into the heart of life itself.

Chapter 5
Every Long Journey Begins With the First Step

One day, I found myself having just finished my shift in a cafe in town. It had been busier than usual, and I felt a little tired. Maybe it was the energy of the place more than the actual work that left me drained. Though the cafe was cozy and most customers friendly and kind, something was missing. I could not really put a finger on what it was exactly, but maybe it was simply the impersonality. Nobody ever did or said anything unusual, not even my coworkers. We all came to work, did and said what customers expected us to, and never even questioned if we felt happy doing so: if we really liked repeating the same sentences over and over only to receive the same answers. Once I asked a woman who looked a little pale and stressed, "how are you feeling today?"

She looked at me with a confused expression, as if to say, "why do you ask me that? You are only supposed to sell me my coffee!" But she regained her composure and replied, "I'm good, thank you."

Maybe she simply felt ashamed that I had seen through her mask of makeup, her strong attempt to prop herself up, and had asked those three words that could have revealed her true feelings. But she waxed confident for a moment, suppressed her own sadness, and failed to reveal to the world exactly what she had really been feeling. It truly takes courage to be vulnerable.

Since that day I never again asked anyone anything out of the usual, unless they started the conversation themselves. I had to wait for an hour to meet a friend of mine I had not seen in a while. It was raining outside, and the clouds were dark and heavy, almost purple in color. While waiting, I pulled out my umbrella and decided to go to the library to escape the rain and cold. The weather was changing. Summer had almost yielded to autumn, and then suddenly in the air a and new smell arrived. Winter. The dampness of rain and cold soaked through my thin summer jacket, and I instantly thought my sodden garments might make me sick. I tried, though, to comfort myself with the knowledge passed down by every doctor, that a flu comes only from a virus and not only from the cold.

The library was almost empty. Maybe people had simply stopped reading books. Or the few who did read them were doing so from their tablets and iPads or listening to them on audio. I began to wonder who even has time any more to sit down and read a book. I began noticing that everybody was becoming so busy, and all information was moving so quickly that everything else could catch up with people's attention and keep them engaged. I noticed that articles must be brief and precise, with catchy headlines. Otherwise, people would not bother reading them. It is the same syndrome we encounter in the food we generally consume. White bread, refined sugar, easy carbohydrates, all to support our racing metabolisms, busy schedules, and stressful lives.

I began noticing an emerging movement reclaiming slow-living. Everything from walking slowly, to eating slowly, to talking slowly, and to basically doing anything to slow down the pace of life.

I began noticing people starting to become victims of trying to keep up with the pace of modern living, to suffer from stress, unable to function at all, with anxiety and all sorts of psychological problems from trying to be like everybody else. I noticed that one day, though, they began to wake up. Questions erupted in their minds: why, and for what? Why should we spend our entire lives running toward our own deaths, only to die before we had ever lived? And with this new awareness they started claiming back their lives. They become spiritual teachers or yoga instructors, helping others to live in the moment, insisting that past and future are only mental constructions, that every ambition is only a production of the ego. They began teaching that to gain new insight, one simply has to sit down, close the eyes, and wait. They found that repeating a mantra can be helpful in this process. And with this new recipe for life, they began to find they could happily let go of everything that previously had made their lives miserable. I started noticing many of my mother's friends going through that process, in all their different colors of being. They would come to visit us over dinner: talking about ancient gods, old, forgotten spiritual traditions, or something else they had recently discovered as a tool on their path to enlightenment. They would gladly share their new insights and cast a light on our mother-daughter duo. One time my mother was told the entire story of a past life she had once lived back in the times of Atlantis. She learned it from a friend of hers who had just started studying down at the clairvoyance school in town. It was a dramatic story and apparently ended up with her being killed when a wild horse kicked her in the stomach, right at her liver. That was why she suffered so much with her health in this life. Maybe it was really true, or maybe this woman, like many others, was falling victim to her own imagination. Nevertheless, my mother would listen, interested, thinking that maybe one day she could use some of this in one of her new novels.

Maybe like in her novel, I would meet one of her friends at the library, and I would look around. But the building would be almost empty except for a few young people playing computer games on the public computers and a few older men reading newspapers quietly.

I ventured over to the section of history books, where I found the shelf about ancient civilizations. I looked through the selection, and there it was, the book I had been looking for: *Egypt from the Pyramids Till Today*, written by an English historian and archeologist. I glanced at my watch and realized that time had again run faster than my sense of it. I hurried to the main hall of the library to register the book in my name before heading off to meet my girlfriend.

I thereafter met my friend Sofie in a cafe in the main square. Shortly after we sat down, I said, "I want to go to Egypt." She looked surprised, because with her I had never shared many stories about my father.

"Really? All alone?" she asked.

"Yes. Alone. I want to look for my father; not that I really believe he is still alive. He would be almost in his eighties by now, an accomplishment for anyone from his part of the world, but at least I want to try to know my roots and feel the warm desert sand beneath my feet."

"But is it even safe to go there alone as a traveler? Maybe you should ask one of these television programs that look for lost family members for help," she suggested. "It will be cheaper for you as well."

She was overflowing with questions and suggestions. She even offered to come along if I needed her company. I told her, though, that I wanted to go on this adventure alone. I wanted to explore and see where the road would take me, to follow my inner compass and callings for a while and hopefully meet my destiny on the way, or at least some parts of it.

We remembered a class we had both attended back in high school about the Arab Spring and the attempts to take back freedom from oppressive regimes. Then the topic slowly changed more to human rights and the suppression of women still happening in large parts of the world.

"I will be careful, of course. So as not to draw too much attention and all of that. Once I'm out in the villages I'll wear a shawl around my head like Muslim women," I assured her.

We sat quietly. I thought about the adventure I wanted to go on, and Sofie probably about her next assignment at the university. She was studying sustainable science and had been one of my best friends since childhood. We always attended the same schools and lived in the same area. She always knew there was something unsettled inside me, something not fully satisfied with reality as it was here. And because I hadn't approved of her decision to attend the university, I would have to look for my destiny elsewhere.

"I think it's a good idea," she said. "Maybe there you'll find everything you are looking for inside, and when you come back, everything will look the same here as always."

It felt good to have her blessings, and a place and friend to return to on the other side of my journey. We sat in the cafe for another few hours, talking about everything under the Sun. Once we were ready to leave, the rain finally stopped, and I could go home on my bicycle and tell my mother about my new plans. I was too excited about the adventure ahead, though, to care the slightest about their complaints. My mother, who also thought it was a good idea, helped me obtain a fake vaccination card from a friend of hers. She insisted that vaccines had caused her a lot of her health issues. So, she had forbidden me to ever have any. She had even written articles about the dangers of vaccinations and what consequences they could possibly have for some.

There had been a huge increase of polio in Africa after they introduced a new oral vaccine to small infants. It was truly a scandal. Were these preventing us from life itself? Surely some vaccines could save lives, but nobody looked at what happens to one's general health after receiving them: the long-term consequences of ingredients such as mercury and aluminum on the body. I had read that the Coronavirus vaccine was beginning to present a health scandal like no other.

Before traveling in many foreign lands, however, one needs to receive hepatitis and yellow fever shots, but my fake yellow vaccination card looked exactly like the real ones I had seen, so I felt confident that all would be in perfect order. In case I got sick out there, I would have to find some wise healer in the desert who could treat me as they had for centuries and centuries, before modern medicine.

Once, my mother told me a story about how my father fell ill from malaria while traveling in Africa. In his youthful longing for freedom, he had gone on a Land Rover journey, traveling with no money all the way from Denmark to South Africa. He crossed borders a foreigner had never crossed and slept surrounded by wild animals. Yet he never felt any fear. Perhaps he mastered and overcame his fears. He had been trained as a medical doctor in Cairo and was able to treat many patients along the way. Everywhere, he was greeted with warm welcomes. In return he received food and a bed and lived with tribes in hidden parts of Africa, drinking goat blood for breakfast and in the evenings dancing around fires to the hypnotic throb of traditional music. One day he woke up burning with a high fever. He had been traveling with a Dutch fellow, who also fell ill. Not long afterward they were with severe malaria. They had to go to the next city to be treated in a hospital. The doctors there instantly wanted to put them on medication. The Dutchman accepted. A few days later he was found dead in his bed. My father refused to take the medication. He just wanted to let the fever burn itself out so he could return to his own health. When this did not happen and he was almost on his death bed, all the doctors and staff there thought him to be an utterly lost cause. He had paid a lot of money for staying at the hospital. When they wanted to transport him to a new place to be treated, he agreed on doing so and paid them even more. On his way, he suddenly realized they were only taking him to a hospice facility to die, cheating him out of the last of his money.

He became so angry about such disrespect for his humanity that a feeling of injustice made him sit up for the first time in a few days. He managed to get them to stop the car. He got out of the car and walked away, only to pass out a little further down the road. When a passerby found him and put him in a bed, he began healing. His anger and feelings of injustice had been so powerful that they almost caused him to rise from the dead. I hoped the same thing would not happen to me on my journey, but I felt good to know there were many kinds of medicine in this world.

I was busy preparing for my journey — buying a few things I needed such as some summer clothing that would not reveal too much skin, which is considered inappropriate in most parts of the Arab world. I never had much time to open the book I'd borrowed from the library. But one afternoon I found some time just to sit in bed and look through the pages of photos and descriptions of the pyramids, temples in southern Egypt, and the hidden treasures of Tut-ankh Amon's tomb. The latter had been found completely intact by an English archeologist back in 1915. He, as well as most people present at the opening of the tomb for the first time since the death of Tut-Ankh Amon in 1323 BC, died from lung problems within a few years. Evidently, modern humans have no resistance to some ancient microbes.

There were images of the valley of the kings, images of entire tunnels covered with stories unfolding in the language of hieroglyphics and colors carved into the walls. These ornaments had taken hundreds of slaves years and years to make. As soon as a new pharaoh would come to power, he would begin preparing his death tomb: more spacious, more glorious, and more powerful than ones of the previous ruler.

To me, this all sounded strange to spend so much time preserving a dead body, to leave all their wealth in a dark hole in the ground along with their preserved body. Did they hope that a long time in the future, someone would find them so their stories would live on and never be forgotten?

I guess if that is what they intended, they truly succeeded. Or perhaps through mummification they hoped the people of the future would have found a cure for death, and by that time they could be brought back to life. I was shocked upon reading an article in a magazine of evolutionary science about how people today suffering from incurable illnesses pay immense sums to be put into a freezer while they are still alive, hoping to be unfrozen when medicine finds a cure for their condition and wake up. I was shocked to read that these things were actually possible and had started happening.

The images in the book impressed me with the beauty of ancient Egyptian architecture. How, without modern technology, they managed to construct such buildings. Truly, we must have been far more developed as humans in the past than we often assume. Beauty and symbolism were everywhere to find in ruins, remains, and artifacts. It seemed that they lived in perfect harmony with nature. They understood the miracle of the Sun, worshipped it, and called it Rah, the God that gives life to all living things. They prayed and thanked Earth for bringing food and the clouds for bringing rain to make everything come alive. They truly understood the cycle of life, how nothing can exist without the other, how the Sun without the rain would make everything wither, how the rain without the Sun would drown everything, and how only together, Earth, Air, Sun, and Water could make life magically appear everywhere and in all forms. They seemed truly to have understood the miracle of life.

I thought about the ugly skyscraper they had just finished down at the harbor in my city: a cold, gray, cement-colored building offering nothing of beauty for the human eye. Is this really the best we can do in response to the architectural wonders of the ancient Egyptians? I thought it terribly sad. Now we think only about building as conveniently, quickly, and inexpensively as possible. But what happened to beauty and aesthetics? Are we not touched deeply inside when we travel south to see one of those beautiful twelfth-century cathedrals honoring the beauty of God and His creation? They took centuries to build, requiring the labor of thousands.

I thought about how today's shopping malls have become our new churches and God has become the sum of our purchases. Many think that the more they buy, the happier they will become. Beauty has been replaced by glamour. Our innate quest for freedom has become a hunger for money. The more money we have, the freer we think we become. But either illness or death will eventually knock on our door and show us that all of this can vanish in an instant.

I had to pull myself away from these thoughts, because they made me feel hopeless. They made me consider that perhaps my way of thinking was too judgmental. Maybe I was not yet wise enough to embrace a grander picture of evolution.

I put my attention back onto the book in front of my eyes, turned the page, and fell upon an entire chapter about the Goddess Isis. She was one of the most popular Goddesses in Egyptian history and has been worshipped widely through the centuries. Her popularity among present-day enthusiasts of the neo-pagan movement was inherited from Afghanistan. Her name means "throne," and she had been a queen of a dynasty lasting from 2465 until 2325 BC. She was also a magical healer. She cured the sick and brought the deceased back to life. She became a role model for all woman. Her image in the book shows her as beautiful, wearing a dress bearing either a hieroglyphic sign or a symbol of the Sun, and always with cow horns atop her head.

Isis became the symbol of powerful womanhood.

I began to feel deeply enchanted by these stories. They touched somewhere inside my deep womanly nature. As I read on further, I saw how much Islam and all else that followed from Mohammod on the mountain had suppressed and forgotten the Feminine. The power and beauty of woman has become completely hidden by burkas and shame. The entire Islamic world has become unjustly dominated by men. How could that have happened? Because of the Koran's statements about woman? Or did it come simply from interpretations of the Koran? I remembered seeing a documentary about Syria from back in the forties, when women still wore their hair loose and exposed their legs to the Sun. Today, in most parts of the Islamic world, such behavior would be unthinkable except among the wealthy. Money has a way of buying God out and buying women clout. If you have enough money, why would you need Him? Isn't the Koran the same now as then, I thought.

I thought of how in the Islamic world, women have served mainly as tools to keep house and produce children, myriads of children. Every child is a blessing from Allah, proclaims the Koran. No population in history has expanded as greatly in such a short time as the Muslim population. In the 1960s they totaled only 27 million, whereas today they have almost reached almost 100 million. I found this incredible. Where did all these souls come from? Has the survival rate simply become higher, the quality of life better, the blessings of Allah more and more frequent? My eyes started to feel heavy, so I decided to put the book aside and take a little nap.

A few hours later I was awakened by a knock on my door. Mother! She was worried about me because I was being so quiet in my room. I looked at my watch and discovered to my surprise that I had slept for three hours. Maybe the rain and cold weather had made me sick after all. Virus or no virus, I got out of bed. It was time for dinner, and outside it was already starting to get dark. My mother was in the kitchen with Aunt Clara, preparing dinner.

I hadn't seen my aunt for a long time, so I was happy. She gave me a big hug. A few years ago, she and her family had moved to an island. Since then, we saw her only a few times a year. She and my mother would speak on the phone almost every day.

"How are you, darling?" she asked. "I hear you are going to

Egypt in a few weeks. Your mother just told me. Should I be worried?" she asked with a smile.

All I could say was that I hoped not. She understood because both she and my mother had traveled widely in their youth. Sometimes together, sometimes alone. Both had spent the years of their twenties traveling across every part of India and Nepal, looking for their destiny in ashrams, temples, and on the roads while meeting others on the same quest. They traveled by rustic local trains to villages that had never seen a person with white skin. Always, my mother would tell the same story of how a small girl in southern India had come up to her and started trying to scrape off my aunt's skin with her finger. She felt sure she would be dark underneath. The world was different back then: more unexplored and less global and interconnected than today.

The internet has changed the world more rapidly than anything else. But still there remain a few corners where people still live within their old cultural traditions, speak only their own language, eat only what the land provides, and live happily, not knowing what else is out there. I was hoping I would find such places on my journey.

Often when people live apart from the rest of the world, they live by means of a different wisdom. They know every single corner of the land. The stars are their traffic lights. The Sun is their only watch. They are born into nature, living with nature, and they know their entire existence depends on her. So, they respect her. Worship her. Care for her. Sing songs and perform offerings to her. And when they become ill, they know how to heal with herbs and prayers and by connecting themselves to the source of all life. When someone is about to die, they all gather to follow and assist the dying on the journey ahead. At least this is how I imagined it all to be like.

"When is your flight and what are you going to do when you get there?" my aunt asked.

I felt a little ashamed of flying because I knew that Mother Earth was paying a heavy price for this kind of pollution, but my aunt assured me this calculation was not so simple.

"You also owe Mother Earth to go and see the amazing and diverse landscapes she has created. How abundant and rich this planet is," she said with a smile.

Maybe she was talking just as much to herself, because my aunt's whole family was going to spend a three-week Christmas vacation on a beach in Costa Rica. She had always wanted to improve her Spanish, so signed up the whole family for a one-week intensive Spanish course.

"I'm thinking about finding an Arabic course in Cairo. Just as a beginning, because most people don't really speak English very well. It could be helpful for me to know some basics," I said. "Or maybe I will just try to make friends with some locals and see what I can pick up along the way."

"That is a brilliant idea! You can learn a little from your mother, also."

"You never told me you spoke Arabic!" I said, looking surprised.

"Not really," she assured me. "Only a few words. Enough to buy a few things at the market or to ask for directions, but never enough to really talk about anything of importance."

"Why didn't you try to learn more from my father?"

"I was lazy and naive. I already spoke English fluently, so I simply didn't bother to really try to learn it. It's one of the most difficult languages in the whole world to learn."

"Even more difficult than Danish?"

"Far more!"

I felt a little exhausted internally because I knew quite a few foreigners and had seen how much they struggled to learn our language.

That evening we all sat around the table in our little wooden house and ate dinner together, just like when I was a child and my aunty was living with us for long periods of time. I felt safe and happy to be with both of them, for I often missed my aunt. When she met her husband, who was a sustainable agriculture engineer, she happily left the city to help him out with a project in the countryside. A few years later they married, bought an old farm on an island, restored the farm, and turned it into a retreat place where my aunt could offer her dance and meditation workshops. She had found her calling in life by teaching people to free themselves through dance. Her workshops became more and more popular. The pressures and stress of modern living had increased the need for a remedy. Almost all of her workshops were filled. Everyone left feeling more in harmony than ever.

We spent almost every summer on the farm, my mother and I. I played with my cousins, who were only a few years younger. My mother helped my sister out with her workshops, preparing food from the farm and helping out with accommodations and all sorts of details. And because we didn't have much money to travel to more exotic places, we usually spent our summers there. I loved it all! Those warm summer evenings just before bed, when we would all bike down to the beach to jump in the ocean, wait for the Sun to set over the wide-open blue blanket of water, and ride back to close our eyes just in time for the first stars to show. What else could one ask for?

Sometimes my oldest aunt and her husband would visit there too, and the whole family would be gathered around the table, eating, sharing, and laughing. Those days were full of loveliness and levity. I loved my oldest aunt as well, and she taught me many great manual skills. She was a full-time designer, working for various international companies as well as weaving her own brand of furniture fabrics.

Of course, when we were all together, as with most families, conflicts and old fights could also be a part of everyday life. But in the end, your heart chooses which memories you wish to carry with you.

I received a big hug from my aunty that night before she left. She wished me all the best of luck on the journey and asked me to send a postcard from the pyramids, only because she knew my mother had never seen them despite her many visits to Egypt. I promised her to come back in one piece, to bring with me some oriental spices, and to generally send her some warm winds from the desert. I told her I would bring her a whole pyramid if I could, and we all laughed at the thought of picking up a pyramid at the airport baggage claim counter.

Chapter 6
Arriving in a New World

From the airport, calling my friend Sophie, I said, "if I don't come back, you can have all my clothing." She laughed, agreed, and said she hoped I wouldn't come back then. We both laughed. I hung up the phone and was now alone. I had checked in my backpack at the Egypt Air counter, hugged my mother farewell in the departure hall, gone through security, and was now waiting for my gate to show on the screen of departing flights. I felt fabulous: as if I had the whole world with all its extraordinary beauty and potential awaiting me to finally come along and discover whatever it had been preparing for me. I generally had the feeling that what you seek is somehow also searching for you, like forces of attraction in the world. All I had to do was trust in that feeling more, then the rest would just come. I was sitting there talking to myself mentally, and so didn't even notice that the gate number of the flight had come up. I followed the arrows to Gate 13.

It was a small airport, so it took only a few minutes to get to the gate. The area was already half-full with passengers, but I found a bench and sat next to a man I estimated to be in his fifties. He was busy on both his phone and his computer. He wore a tight suit, a nice white, newly ironed shirt, and a bow tie. I thought he must be a real business man, probably he lived half of his life in airports and the other half in hotel rooms around the world. I wondered if he was happy. I concluded that he probably didn't even have time to ask himself such questions. I directed my thoughts elsewhere.

I had flown only a few times before, so the whole feeling of airports was a bit new to me. I felt unsettled by having to transfer flights in Frankfurt, apparently the largest airport in all of Europe. I tried to comfort myself by thinking that, as with most things in life, we learn only by doing, so it is best to relax as much as possible. I leaned my back against the bench and closed my eyes.

The flight went smoothly, and the next thing I felt was hot, thick, humid air as I stepped out the door of the Cairo airport terminal.

How can anyone even breathe here, I thought.

The air was thick with pollution blended with some sweet smell—a mix of spices and flowers? What a strange smell! But maybe every place, country, and continent has its unique odor. I remembered the fragrance of orange blossoms in southern Spain, the etheric, fresh, thin mountain air of the Swiss Alps, and the scent of wet soil on rainy days back in Denmark.

The terminal was packed. Some waited, holding signs bearing names of relatives or loved ones. A line of eager taxi drivers each eyed me as their best target. Lightheaded and dizzied by all the simultaneous offers, after a moment I just agreed to go with the nearest driver. I handed him a little hand-written note with an address: Old Cairo Hotel, Zahir Road, Raban Bazar. I asked him to take me there. I didn't even care about the price or if he cheated me. All I wanted was to get to the hotel room I'd booked from home and sleep a whole night before taking in any more impressions.

"Old Cairo?" he asked in heavily accented English. I nodded. He flicked the butt of his cigarette on the ground, yelled something to one of his taxi-driver buddies, threw my suitcase in the trunk, climbed in the car, and off we went as the taxi drivers yelled and whistled at him.

I had booked a cheap hotel in the old center of Cairo. Because I didn't know the city at all, I didn't know what to expect. My mother had warned me about Cairo being the most chaotic and relentless place she had ever visited. She swore she would rather die than live there. She often exaggerated, though, and because I knew her sensitive nature, I had not fully believed her until now. From the airport to the hotel, it took two full hours of driving through the most hellish traffic I had ever suffered. A five-lane road branched off in all directions from a roundabout encircling the entire city. Traffic rules were clearly nonexistent with no traffic lights, and with honking the only way of jousting for position. Did my driver even have a license? I was so shocked by the harsh reality suddenly in my face that when I finally reached my hotel, I felt lucky just to still be alive. I hurried out of the car, gladly forking over the bills for the surely overpriced ride.

I was relieved when greeted in English by an older gentleman who had welcomed hundreds of thousands of other tourists dazed by the shock of their first arrival. He checked me in instantly, directing me to a room with a towel and a shower. He told me he could arrange some dinner if I was hungry. I thanked him and told him that all I needed was sleep.

I was out the second my head hit the pillow.

The next morning, I felt as rested as a completely new person, even though I had been awakened several times by prayers erupting from the mosque. The call to prayer started around four o'clock, followed by a mix of prayers and songs broadcasted through loudspeakers every second hour during the day to remind everyone who believes in Allah about His glory. I showered, put on some appropriate clothing, then looked through my jewelry box and found the necklace from my mother. I put it on and left my room feeling ready to meet the world outside.

First, though, I needed some breakfast. I was starving after only having eaten flight food the day before.

"Good morning, sunshine," came a deep voice from behind the reception desk.

It was the same man who had checked me in yesterday.

"Did you sleep well?" he asked.

I told him I'd slept like a princess, and now all I could think about was to have something to eat. He introduced himself as Muhammad, like the prophet. He was the owner of the hotel, which had been his pride since he himself arrived here almost thirty years before. He told me I could ask him anything I needed and he would do his very best to help me. He was a kind man, and I instantly felt comfortable and safe in his company. He showed me to the restaurant hall, where there awaited a breakfast buffet. He passed me over to a young waiter before telling me to come see him at reception for a map before going outside.

A few minutes later, I sat down at my restaurant table with a plate full of food that smelled and looked foreign compared to anything I was used to. A few dishes such as hummus and baba ganoush were not new to me. But for breakfast?

The main dish was a large pot of something I had never seen. Foul: A Traditional Egyptian Breakfast Dish, a sign announced invitingly in front of the warm, streaming pot. It was full of brown beans in a tomato sauce, topped with fresh onions, fresh chopped coriander leaves, and a sprinkle of olive oil.

It was really tasty, especially for dipping delicious Egyptian flat bread. The waiter told me the name of the bread in Arabic was Aish Baladi. I tried for a second to really imprint that in my mind, but knew I would soon forget because of all the new things at once. I filled another plate with nicely crispy falafels and some tahini to dip them in.

I usually didn't take coffee in the morning, but the waiter convinced me I really had to try his deliciously spicy Arabic variety.

"Best coffee in the whole world," he promised me.

So, I agreed on trying one, maybe mostly to not upset him. But it was truly as delicious as promised, I had to admit. A strong rich coffee flavor, a spice I instantly identified as cardamom, but too sweet with all the added sugar. Still, I drank and thought that perhaps I would need the energy later. When I finished eating, I went to Muhammad to pick up the map.

"Don't leave the area of Old Cairo, okay?" he warned me. "It is crazy out there, and nothing much to see except for skyscrapers, malls, compounds, and traffic going in all directions."

I made him a promise to stay within the area, and he pointed out a few places on the map worth visiting: some beautiful old Islamic architecture, a bazaar area worth doing some shopping at, and a few restaurants where one could sit in peace and quiet and very likely meet other westerners. He wrote me a note with his phone number and the address of the hotel and told me in case I got lost I could always call him.

I left the hotel lobby and walked out on the street. The Sun was already burning, even though it was not even ten o'clock yet, and the air was hazy from all the pollution and traffic dust. The streets were still quite empty, with only a few locals bringing out groceries to display or opening up their shops. I walked down the street and turned left at the next corner, and as Muhammad explained, entered a narrower road, crossed at a traffic light, and entered the area of old Islamic architecture.

The buildings were beautiful, full of detail, symmetry, and symbolism. Every corner and edge had been thought about and crafted with materials used for decades. They looked nothing like what we build today. I was astonished. I took some photos on my phone from a few different angles, trying to capture the essence of the place. As I walked around, a few people stopped me, asked my nationality, my name, whether I liked Egypt or not, if I was going to the pyramids, and if I needed a taxi or a bus. The questions were endless. People were generally friendly and simple, though some tried to push me to come into their shops and buy something. They were not happy to let me go when I wanted, so I learned quickly that sometimes you have to be a little strong and clear, without coming off as too unfriendly. Some men stared at me because I was wearing my hair loose and my skin was whiter than most. They would throw a kiss in my direction and say things like "hey baby".

Because of all of the suppression on women, you do not see many females on the streets in these areas. They are at home cooking, taking care of children, and watching television, and if they ever come out, you see only a narrow line of face revealing the two eyes. Otherwise, the women remain completely covered, face and body, often in black. When a woman with a child passed me in a burka of thick black material, I imagined how overbearingly hot it must feel.

In more affluent areas, things were different. Women roamed much more freely, wearing clothing like mine. But in these parts, it was really considered unthinkable for a woman to show any of herself. One could argue that a certain sacredness around a woman, now lost in the West, still exists in these parts. Still, the women were not free to choose their own destinies.

I knew I had to be careful in some areas and at certain times of day, because many there had the impression that white women were somehow loose: that because they do not follow the rules of the Koran, they can never go to heaven anyways. So why not try to spend a night with them? These are the kinds of tendencies you'll see in many countries where sexuality has been extremely suppressed for centuries, as in the Arab world. One result of such repression is that porn is more popular in the Arab world than in all other places. The more something is forbidden, the more exciting it becomes. And when many humans break free from the suppression of Islam, they start worshipping their plastic surgeon instead of Allah. They go from one extreme to another. Now all they can think about is their looks and how to flaunt them in the most obvious ways.

The pendulum swings back and forth from repression to lubricity, before at some point finding a perfect balance in the middle.

I remembered a story I had read on Facebook. It was about the wealthiest man in all of Cairo. He could simply not be happy until he married the most beautiful girl in all of the Arab world, so she could bring him children and happiness. He searched for her far and wide, finally finding her in Beirut, asking for her hand, and bringing her to his palace in Cairo. They were happy at first. He had all the money in the world, and she could go shopping for all the things she ever dreamed of, eat the most luxurious meals, and drink the finest drinks. Shortly after, she became pregnant and bore him his first son, but as the child grew a little older, the husband soon realized to his disappointment that the child had not inherited any of his mother's beauty. They had one more child, but the same thing happened. This time it was a girl, and she looked nothing like her mother. Then one more son arrived, who was even uglier than the first two. The husband started to feel a little suspicious. He researched her background and found that to look the way she did she had submitted herself to the plastic surgeon's knife at least twenty times. He became furious and felt so cheated that he divorced her and then sued her for what he considered to be fraud. The article did not reveal whether he won the case or not, but I found the whole story to be hilarious. Of course, I thought it was fully his own fault and quite ironic. Genetics do not lie. Maybe one can buy beauty, but never true love.

I turned down a little narrow street and entered the bazaar area that Muhammad had told me about. 'Rajab Risk Bazaar Treasures of Egypt', announced an imposing sign at the entrance. It was exactly the place I had been looking for. I felt good inside about my navigation skills having taken me so far. The place was chaotic, the streets narrow, and one shop extended right into the next, with people everywhere wearing a vast array of colorful shawls and clothing, jewelry and gemstones. There were also heaps of spices and Egyptian souvenirs. I felt as if I had just entered a market back in Persian times, and that soon the smell of incense and spices would hypnotize me completely and erase any other reality.

I instantly loved it and tried to allow myself to get carried away with all the colors and scents. I went into a few shops and bought a pair of earrings and a soft pashmina shawl. The young trader told me his shop used to be his father's, and before his father's it has been his grandfather's, and that one day his son would take over.

So easy and simple to just be born into one's destiny, I thought to myself. Not like in the West, where the endless possibilities of what to do and who to become often end up leaving young people in a stage of absolute confusion and paralysis. The paradox of choice. They end up stunned by the freedom and anxious about making the wrong decision. They end up never committing to anything because the choices are simply too many. So often we humans strive for freedom, but do we even know what to do with it when we have it?

Being born into one's profession would save one from so many thoughts about identity and so much confusion, I thought as I thanked the owner of the shop and left feeling pleased with my new purchases. Despite all the challenges, I did feel grateful to be able to choose my own path in life.

Back in the chaos of the crowded narrow streets with their endless jewels and colors, I realized that all these new impressions had really started to make me hungry. I pulled out the map, took a few minutes to orientate myself, and began walking toward one of the cafes Muhammad had pointed out. It was a long walk.

The room was thick with hazy smoke from the many sitting around tables in the almost full cafe, sharing a water pipe among themselves, something very common in these parts of the world. The water pipe, called a *shisha*, holds a mixture of flavored tobacco and molasses sugar. The tobacco is heated with charcoal, and the heat pushes the smoke into a water container, where it bubbles through before leaving through a hose. It is then inhaled. I remembered that my aunt had one in her apartment when I was young. I think she used it quite a lot when she was really young, but now would never dream of ever putting anything like that into her body. All the dancing workshops and Buddhist meditation retreats had made her so clean inside that she might become sick just standing next to anyone smoking a cigarette at a bus stop.

She would claim so whenever the whole smoking topic would occasionally surface.

Now for the first time I really believed her. The room was so thick with smoke and the aroma of all the pipes that one surely did not need to smoke to partake of the effects. It is cheaper to remain a passive smoker anyway, I thought. I found an empty table closest to the window. A waiter brought me the menu, and I ordered some Lebanese Rice rolls in wine leaves and some hummus with bread.

It felt good to sit down after all the hours of walking around and exploring all the new places. Crowds of people have always made me tired, and for a second in that smokey cafe room I wished to just be alone in nature, away from all the noise and people, but I had to be strong and remember my purpose for coming: to try to find out what had really happened to my father and to see and feel the spirit of the place that was a part of my journey into this world long before I arrived myself. Every place in this world somehow has its own soul, I came to learn.

I pulled out a little piece of paper from my handbag. My mother had written out the address of the apartment where my father's sister and husband had once lived: Rasha & Nabil. 27 al Mansour St, Apartment 8, Heliopolis.

When the waiter brought the food, I had asked him how far Heliopolis was. He kindly replied that it could be reached by taxi within twenty minutes. I did not know if the address would lead me anywhere, but I did not have much other information except the name of another brother who, according to my mother, lived permanently in an old Beirut apartment once owned by their family before they had lost their entire fortune. One of these days I would go there and take a look, but for now I just wanted to be a traveler for a while and explore the world, eat the delicious new food, and take in all I could of these strange smells and sounds coming from every direction.

I finished eating the last food from my plate, paid the bill, and walked back to my hotel to rest for a few hours.

The restaurant lobby was almost full as I entered for dinner that evening. All the tables were taken, and the waiter apologized sincerely and informed me that a lot of people had come to eat from outside because the day was a special Islamic day of celebration. Apparently, there are many.

He asked me to wait and said he would ask Mr. Smith if I could sit at his table. He went to a table in the far corner of the restaurant to ask a man I could see only from behind.

The waiter returned and told me it would be a pleasure for Mr. Smith if I would join him. He asked me what I would like to drink, and I asked him for a tea with some herbs. He told me he would make me an infusion of anise. My stomach was a little unsettled from all the new food and bacteria, but everybody told me these symptoms would pass within a short time when my system had time to adjust to its new environment. I filled a plate with grilled eggplant, a dish of couscous and green beans, some bread, and a bowl of tahini to dip it all in. Then I walked over to the table in the corner, where this Mr. Smith was sitting.

"I was told I could sit here at your table because the whole place is full," I said a little shyly, maybe because he was rather handsome, and because I hadn't really made anything of my appearance apart from putting on my new earrings. I suddenly felt very self-conscious.

"Good evening," he said in a calm and friendly tone of voice. "You are more than welcome."

I felt a little calmer as I sat down opposite him and took the first bite from my plate.

"What's your name?" he asked.

"Alanna," I replied, with more confidence than the sentence before.

"Ah, that's a special name," he replied thoughtfully.

I tried to identify his accent, but couldn't really hear if he was Irish, Scottish, or even English.

"And yours?"

"Michael, but call me Mike, everybody does."

He asked for my nationality and told me he was born in Edinburgh but grew up in the Welsh countryside, so my judgement had not been completely off, which made me feel even further relieved. He seemed confident and sure about himself as he tried to start a conversation about traveling sites in Egypt. He then realized I had just arrived the day before.

"What brings you here all alone?" he asked. "Egypt is not really a place for a young woman like you to backpack," he added.

I was starting to feel good in his company. Something in his being had a very calming and grounding effect on me, so I told him about what I knew about my father and why I had come here hoping to at least find out more.

"That is beautiful," he said after I finished telling him the last details of what I knew. "I hope your seeking will get you somewhere. One should never stop exploring this world and all its mysteries. Every time I know something new it only brings me to realize further all that I still don't know, and hidden behind every answer awaits another thousand questions."

He seemed quite sure of himself. Calm, in control, and not so much affected by the confusions of life as the rest of us. Every move, gesture, and word seemed to come from a place of tranquility and certainty. I concluded that maybe he had simply just lived a little longer than me. He told me he was working as a freelance journalist and blogger and had just come back from Sinai, where he had been writing an article about how the terror attack on a tourist bus a few years back had changed tourism and how many camps and hotels had been forced to shut down afterwards because nobody dared to go there any more.

The Taba bus bombing had been given many names. The tourist coach bus was parked, waiting to cross the border into Israel from Egypt, when a lone suicide bomber entered and detonated his explosives. Four people were killed and seventeen injured. Why is it often the few who ruin it for the rest of us?

It is truly a sad story. He told me the area is now utterly packed with security guards and police officers, checking all luggage and belongings every five kilometers. That proves to be quite exhausting traveling by car.

He told me that Sinai was incredibly beautiful. The colors of nature were like nowhere else he had ever seen: pastel landscapes and horizons, and where the sea meets the horizon, you feel almost as if heaven were meeting Earth. He also mentioned that the bottom of the ocean was filled with coral reefs, which made it a true paradise for divers.

The Sinai Peninsula, or half island, is a part of Egypt located in Asia. It is situated between the Mediterranean Sea to the north and the Red Sea to the south and has long served as a land bridge between Asia and Africa. It is the home of the biblical site Mount Sinai, where Moses was believed to have spoken with God himself on that mountain. I remembered that my mother and father had once climbed to its summit. Due to the geographical location, Sinai had for centuries been the center of conflicts, and for long periods of history Sinai, like the rest of Egypt, had been occupied and controlled by foreign empires. It had been occupied by Israel since 1967 and was given back to Egypt in 1979 as the result of an Israel-Egypt peace treaty. It had for many years been a huge tourist attraction, especially for Christians who hoped to come and see for themselves the famous biblical burning bush, or at least to walk in the footsteps of Moses for a while. Mike told me he had been there several times over the past years and that the eastern coast was definitely the most beautiful. All the way down along the coast, one can find natural campsites with huts and cottages made of bamboo or palm leaves, right on the beach. You can wake up to the sunrise every morning, walk a few steps, and dive straight into the water for a morning swim. In the evenings, the people of the camp gather around a fire, play music, share stories, and make food.

"I don't know exactly what it is," Mike said, "but there are forces there that draw you back time after time. I always think it will be my last visit there, but then a few years later I will find myself back again. Maybe it's just a good place to come and reflect and gather one's whole being."

It was nice talking with him. I instantly felt pleasant in his company. Maybe age had brought him some inner tranquility, unlike the men or boys I knew back home. I had just finished the last sip of my anise tea when Mike told me he would go and try to sleep early, because tomorrow he would have to go downtown (the busiest area of all of Cairo) to try to find a camera shop where two years before, he had borrowed a lens from the shop owner and not managed to pay the guy back yet. He thanked me for the company, told me he would be around for a few more days, and that I would surely see him the next day.

I also felt tired, went to my room, and tried to read a little from the *Lonely Planet* guidebook I brought from home, but my eyelids kept falling, so I put the book away and just as I had the day before, slept the moment my head hit the pillow.

Chapter 7
A Taste of Love

Over breakfast the next morning, I once again looked at the paper bearing the address of my father's sister, my aunt, and her husband. I was contemplating whether I should get a taxi and go there today or not. Something inside felt unsettled about it, possibly the fear of disappointment, which could end up ruining the whole purpose of my trip. Or perhaps I simply just needed a little more time to adjust to my new surroundings and enjoy the freedom of being out traveling on my own.

I asked Muhammad about what to do and what to see, and he told me to go and take in a famous old mosque called the Ibn Tulun. It is both the largest and oldest mosque in all of Africa. I got myself ready, packing a bag with a water bottle, a banana, and a shawl to wrap around my head if necessary, then off I went.

A few hours later I found myself back in the hotel lobby, tired from the traffic, the taxi ride, and the relentless burning of the Sun. I decided to rest for a few hours and then see how I would spend the rest of the day. Before I went into my room, I passed by the restaurant to collect some cold drinking water. To my surprise I found Mike there. He was sitting at the same table in the corner and reading a book while enjoying a cup of coffee.

"Hi," he said with a wide smile. "Glad to see you again. How is it going?"

I told him a few details about the beauty of the mosque and then added how exhausting I'd found all the noise, traffic, and the rush of the city. He told me he could not agree more. He also felt drained after spending all morning searching for a specific photography shop he once knew but didn't remember the exact location, only to find out it had closed a few months earlier. Now he was unable to pay back the kind shop owner who so generously had helped him out with the lens. He always rented his own car when he was here, he told me.

"Frankly, people here drive like idiots," he said, "not even realizing they are not only risking their own lives but also those of others. Not to mention the quality of the roads being built here! They are so bad that only a short while after being finished, they collapse because the underlying foundation is too weak. Huge holes in the road begin appearing. It's crazy to think that the people who built the pyramids and temples, which lasted for several thousand years, are the same ones who today build roads that cannot last even two years," he said.

I agreed because I had the same thought about a lot of contemporary construction.

"But these people are probably not the same as those who lived there before. I mean, different souls or spirits, if you know what I mean," I added, feeling a little insecure how he would react to my viewpoint, afraid he would judge me as having read too many New Age books.

But instead, he said, "I think you could be quite right. Come and eat some seafood with me tonight? I know the best restaurant in all of Cairo. They serve the freshest and most tasty fish and shrimps you'll ever taste. It's in an area called Rehab, a little far from here, but we can go in my car, and in this way, you'll also get to see a bit more of the city."

I felt quite happy about being asked. Even though I was vegetarian, I would occasionally eat fish if the quality was good and not all like the polluted farmed fish in the supermarket at home. Fish used to be so good and healthy, but within the last fifty years fish have become quite toxic. Simply because we managed to pollute our oceans to such an extent that they had become toxic to ourselves and the environment. As a result, half of the species simply have not survived. I had to force myself to put all these thoughts away before they became depressing, leaving me unable to do anything good for myself or for the world around me. I agreed on meeting Mike in the lobby at seven, feeling quite happy I would be spending an evening in his company.

I showered, put some fragrant creams on my face and body, put my hair up in a pony tail, and used a little bit of makeup on my eyes, which I usually never bothered to do. I put my new earrings on, which I had bought the other day at the bazaar. I then wrapped a shawl around my neck and chest.

While putting on the cream and jewelry, I realized that I wanted him to find me attractive. I felt a little ridiculous because at twice my age, why would he even be interested in a girl like me? I was sure he had been with plenty of women and could get almost any one he wanted, both because of his looks but also because of his calm and confident personality.

Most women like to feel that a man has some structure, that he is somebody she can lean on. Mike seemed to have achieved a good balance between his feminine and masculine natures. He surely enjoyed a rich spiritual life, while on the outside managing to be strong, clear, and in control in any situation. I felt this from him. Maybe he was too controlled, I had thought for a second over dinner the other night, but then he instantly said something silly and slightly ridiculous, which made me relinquish my judgements. When I came out of my room wearing my nicest clothing and ready to go out for dinner in a new part of town, I found him standing in the entrance hall of the hotel.

"Good evening, madam," he greeted me with a warm smile and some playfulness in his brown eyes.

We walked to his car, which was parked just around the corner from the hotel, paid a young fellow who watched all the cars on the street, then started out. I instantly felt that Mike was a good driver. He maintained a complete overview over the road and could keep an eye on every car around him at the same time. For the first time I felt relaxed driving in Cairo. It was relaxing not to feel as if my life could end at any corner. We drove for almost an hour and a half, passing large neighborhoods and compounds where the rich lived in peace within their own city within the city. Mike told me about how rapidly the city had expanded over the years, and how every time he returned, entirely new cities within cities had been built. The population had expanded by almost a million for every two years he had been away.

"Look," he said, pointing to the left, where a huge sign over an entrance greeted us: New Cairo. They had built a new capital in the city, and Mike swore that only two years ago when he was here last time, the whole area was only desert. "Now more than thirty million people live here. It's one of the largest cities in the world, and if it continues to expand it will soon be the very largest."

We drove for another half hour, passing one area of the city extending into the next. I could not understand how Mike could know where he was going at all, but he seemed to know exactly what he was aiming for. We arrived at a large gate. 'Welcome to Al Rehab', it announced. We drove to the entrance, where several security guards wanted us to show a residential card. Mike, though, spoke a bit of Arabic, got out of the car and talked with one of the officers. I don't know about what, but soon he was back in the car, behind the wheel, and the gate in front of us was open and the guard and officers were waving to us politely through, saying "welcome to Al Rehab, and enjoy your stay."

"What did you tell them?" I asked.

"Ah, nothing specific. I just asked their names, told them mine, how beautiful I found their country to be, and that this evening I wanted to take this beautiful lady in the car out for a magical night in their neighborhood."

Beautiful. He finds me beautiful, then! I couldn't help but smile on the inside.

We parked the car near City Square, walked a hundred meters through a shopping area, and arrived at an open square with cafes and restaurants. Mike headed straight for the fish restaurant at the corner, and I followed gladly, feeling safe that he knew exactly where he was going. A few minutes later we were sitting inside an air-conditioned restaurant. He ordered a specific white fish he told me he loved, and I a portion of shrimps and some white rice in fish sauce. We sat there opposite each other and waited for our food. Suddenly I felt very shy.

"Why are you not married with children and a nice villa?" I asked him out of the blue, and instantly regretted it. Why would I ask him such an annoying question, which I was sure he was exhausted hearing from everyone all the time. Perhaps it was because of my insecurity that I tried to gain control over the situation by maybe nudging him a little out of his.

It didn't seem to have worked at all, though.

He casually replied, "well, life doesn't always go the way we plan, does it? It is always somehow better and worse than we could ever have hoped for. I have loved a few women, and they me, but somehow destiny always changed our paths, and we ended up going in different directions. But I have made peace with being alone now, and to be honest I enjoy my own company and the freedom so much that I'm not sure any more that I could return to an ordinary, routine life."

I could really understand him and thought I might eventually end up feeling exactly like him about life and relationships. He was a traveler by heart, and to try to tame that could cost him his life, I was sure.

"I can work from anywhere in the world, writing articles and papers about things of relevance for the rest of the world, and in a few days, I will go to Alexandria, where I've been hired to write a contemporary article about the old Library of Alexandria."

The library had burned down either by accident or on purpose. The most popular story has it that Caesar set fire to some ships in the harbor, but unfortunately the conflagration spread into the library, and only a few books and scrolls were saved. Since then, more and more evidence has proved that it was actually the Christians who had set it on fire.

According to Mike, they really wanted to destroy all this knowledge because knowledge often threatens those in power, whether secular or religious power. The ancient library had been built in the third century BC, in an attempt to gather all human knowledge in one place. The library was home to more than 70,000 books about everything: mathematics, astronomy, physics, history, and many other topics. It was also a place for scholars to come and do research, to study, and to gain knowledge about the world. They gathered original handwritten scrolls from all over the world, and it is believed to have housed at least one million scrolls, holding knowledge of important events and facts about the past, but nobody really knows the exact extent of the collection. One ruler of Egypt, Ptolemy III, required all visitors coming to the city to surrender all books to the library, and every time a ship sailed into the harbor, librarians would search the ship and take all books and scripts they could find. Then scribes would copy these writings so precisely that the original was kept and the copy given back without the owners even noticing.

Alexandria was a modern city at that time, an international place of trade between East and West because of its geographical location by the sea. It was also one of the largest cities of antiquity. Only Rome surpassed it in size. Alexandria featured a huge harbor, where ships would ferry spices and fabrics from one end of the world to the other. In order to safely lead ships into the harbor and show off the city's wealth, they built a lighthouse that was the tallest manmade building of the ancient world and was later considered one of the world's Seven Wonders.

Alexandria was founded by the city's namesake, Alexander the Great, in 331 BC. The paper Mike was to write for the history magazine back in England related how much Alexandria had changed since then and how much of the ancient world could still be seen there. He was getting paid well for this job, and because he was running a little low on money, it was a good opportunity for him and also good for his reputation to get his name in this history magazine. "Not that he really cared about fame or anything," he added a little nonchalantly.

We sat a little and talked about how much the world had changed through history, how different it must have been to have lived in the past, and what beautiful clothing people used to wear back in the times of the Egyptian dynasties. We talked about everything under the Sun that night, and I told him all about my past, my mother and her bad health, my village, my grandmother, and my aunt Clara.

He told me about his grandfather's farm in the highlands of Scotland, where he used to go every summer, and how his childhood growing up in Edinburgh had been equally beautiful and difficult. We each had a glass of wine. Mike, the designated driver, took a few sips, while I finished my glass rather fast and ordered another one. The wine made me feel relaxed and able to let go of all the barriers I was usually carrying. As it grew dark, we decided to start heading back. We paid the bill and left the restaurant.

I was feeling a little lightheaded from the wine and was walking a little too close to the road as we ambled back to the car. So, when a car veered toward me, Mike grabbed my hand and pulled me back into the walking lane. He held my hand at least a few seconds more than necessary, but as soon as he realized it, he pulled it back a little awkwardly and we walked apart for the last few steps towards the car.

I liked him holding my hand, and wished he would have held it much longer.

That night back at the hotel we politely said goodnight. I thanked him for the dinner and the company. I knew he was leaving for Alexandria the next day and so made him promise not to leave before I had the chance to say goodbye. We stood a little awkward in front of each other for some seconds, as if there was more among us that wanted to be said, but neither of us knew how to. I turned around and walked down the hallway towards my room. Behind me I could hear Mike fumbling with the key, while I kept hoping he could say something more or stop me from going into my own room. But he didn't, so we each went to our own room, closed the door, turned off the light, and went to bed. But I was still wide awake, still feeling a little tipsy and lightheaded from the wine. It felt as if every single cell within me had just awoken from death. I thought I would possibly never be able to sleep again. Of course, I knew why, but I struggled to even admit to myself that I was longing to be with a man only two doors further down the hotel hallway.

Did he feel the same? I couldn't be a hundred percent sure, but certain signs made me feel he had similar sentiments. But maybe also he felt a little ashamed because of me being so much younger.

I'd caught a glimpse of his age on his driver's license when he showed it to one of the officers at the gate to Rebah. Forty-four years old. Not too bad considering I would soon turn twenty-two in another nine months. Soon is relative, anyways. Too many thoughts. I had to do something, so I decided to take a shower and wash from myself all these thoughts and desires, only to find myself back in bed ten minutes later with the exact same feeling as before.

If there was no cure for these things, I might as well do it. I allowed myself to have that thought for the first time. I could go and knock on his door and see if he was still awake like I am. Why not? What do I have to lose? He could reject me; tell me he doesn't want to be with me? Tell me to go back to bed and next time look for a man my own age? I would feel ashamed for a while, but then he would leave for Alexandria the day after and I would probably never see him again, so why would that even matter?

Slowly, my thoughts convinced me I would regret tomorrow if didn't even try, at least. I thought that if I die tomorrow, I would at least have lived to the fullest today. And with a force and a desire inside that felt so powerful that it was almost out of control, I wrapped a shawl around my naked body, quietly opened the door to the hotel lobby, tiptoed down the hallway, and found the door.

I knocked quietly. No reply. I knocked again. Still no reply. I tried the door handle. The door was unlocked. I opened it softly.

"Sorry, I didn't hear you. Did you knock? I'm always wearing earplugs when I'm in the city," he said with a quiet voice.

"May I come in?" I asked, a little ashamed.

"Surely," he said, "I was hoping you would come, but I wanted to leave it up to your freedom to choose if that's what you wanted." We looked at each other a little awkwardly before he pulled a smile and spoke.

"I have desired you from the first moment we met a few nights ago in the hotel restaurant."

I took a deep outward breath as I sat on the edge of his bed. We both smiled at each other a little shyly, then he grabbed me with both arms, and the shawl wrapped around me fell off as he pulled me into bed toward him. The room was dark. We could barely see each other, so we touched, with his warm, strong hands investigating my entire body. I started to let go of all the tension I had felt about the situation and surrender myself to his warm touch.

He knew exactly what he was doing. He must have done it thousands of times before with tons of women, I thought for an instant.

"Stop thinking," he whispered in my left ear, "or else you will ruin the entire experience."

It was as if he could hear my stupid thoughts. He then started kissing me softly, with passion, first on the lips and then later on my entire body. He touched me both softly and more forcefully at the same time, and with a perfect pace and rhythm, as if my body were an instrument he was playing. He touched me in places I had never been touched before, and made me feel things I had never known possible. I felt as if I had not even known my own body until this very moment.

That night we made the most beautiful love I had ever made with anyone. Our bodies were no longer separate and had become one. A complete unity of two people. And for the first time I understood how the body is the perfect vehicle to reach our deepest and most intimate dimensions. I hardly knew him before, but in this moment, it felt as if we had never been apart for one second since the first day of our lives. Time and space did not exist, neither yesterday or tomorrow, only this moment, body against body, until we both reached our ultimate pleasure and I fell asleep in his arms, wishing this night would never have to end.

No words could ever explain what happened, so neither of us tried. We simply slept all night in each other's arms. When I did wake up, I heard a door closing quietly. It was him. He had packed his bags and left. Next to me on the bed was a beautiful note, hand-written on palm leaf paper, with a poem.

We shall not cease from exploration,
and the end of all our exploring
will be to arrive where we started
and know the place for the first time.
~ T. S. Eliot

Underneath, these words: "Thank you for everything. I will never forget your beauty." The signature was simply Mike. No phone number, no address, nothing else.

At first, I felt a little sad to have had him in my arms and then so quickly to have lost him, but then I reminded myself that nothing lasts forever anyway, neither the best moment nor the very worst, luckily.

I felt grateful to have added this magical experience to my story. I remembered how much I always fought to be different from my mother, and here I was, in bed with an older man, not that this was the same situation at all, I tried to convince myself.

So often when we set off with a goal to know certain things, life always ends up blessing us with countless other teachings. So often we have become so fixed on the goal that we end up missing everything in-between. Maybe this whole journey to know my father was also a way for me to understand my mother more, why she had made certain decisions in her life that led her to bring me into this world and raise me the way she had.

Sometimes I would get angry with her about not having tried to look for my father, so I would at least have had the chance to know him before it was too late. At other times I would blame her either for simply having had me when her health was so poor, or for other things that teenage girls use against their mothers.

She always replied calmly, saying, "things are the way they are, Alanna, whether you like them or not. Certain things cannot be changed, so we have to accept them and direct our attention to what we can change. But surely one has to be wise to know the difference."

I think her lifelong battle with her body somehow brought her to accept what she never really managed to change. But now I felt something similar to how my mother probably felt with my father, and how amazing it had been for her to be with somebody who lived, loved, knew the secrets of life, and felt its magic in every cell of his body. Age had only enhanced their understanding of life and beauty, and in the dimension of soul and spirit, these things do not matter.

I stayed in bed for another half an hour, allowing myself to be carried away on a stream of endless thoughts. Finally, I decided to get out of bed, find the shawl I had been wearing from the night before, wrap it around myself, open the door quietly, and look to make sure nobody would see me leaving his room — especially not Muhammad.

I was sure such things were not so appropriate in these parts. Muhammad was a loyal man who had been married to the same woman for forty-two years, as he told me when I paid my bill. Maybe their prejudices about Western women being cheap were actually true, and I had just proven them right once again. How long had I known Mike? Two days exactly. But I was sure he and I had spent at least one lifetime together. So, I certainly waited a long time to meet him again.

For a happy moment, all the time spent with Mike made me forget my purpose of coming to Cairo. I really enjoyed my little romance, but soon reality knocked on my door and made me remember why I had come here. But first, I wanted to just spend the rest of the day basking in the lingering beauty from the night.

I somehow felt changed. More like a woman and less like the girl I used to be. I felt grateful for everything. I knew that tonight before going to sleep, I would close my eyes and whisper a little prayer of gratitude to the whole universe.

Chapter 8
Answers

The next day I asked Muhammad to order me an afternoon taxi. I wanted go to the address in Heliopolis. He called his friend Omar, who agreed to take me in the afternoon, wait for me there, and bring me back again safely. Muhammad told me Omar was a good man and a safe driver. I felt sure he would not overcharge me.

It was still early in the day, so I left the hotel to take a little walk in the area and maybe go back to that restaurant where I had eaten lunch the first day. Maybe I would order some juice or something else refreshing. I walked the same route but noticed different things than before. Everything felt a little more familiar, more intimate.

I had learned to say hello - *'as-salamm'alaykum'* - which actually means something like 'may there be peace upon you', an absolutely beautiful greeting. I also learned to say *'shukran'* - 'thank you'. Probably about the same level of Arabic my mother had spoken, I thought, and decided that moment to put some effort into learning a few new words each day.

I walked toward the same old square I'd passed the other day. It was a little later than last time, and the area was even more crowded. This time with multitudes of homeless people. Why hadn't I noticed something so obvious the other day? Possibly many of them slept in the alleys or down at the nearby train station, only to return to their begging base, along the other hundreds of beggars. I could not possibly give something to all of them, so I had to be guarded when passing through the area. I also wasn't sure if it was even good to give them anything at all, because I had so often heard stories of them being robbed by the others afterwards, or of them spending the money instantly on drugs, alcohol, or cigarettes. I feared I would only feed their addiction and increase their misery even further. I wasn't sure, but my heart told me to give something to every single one of them, especially to those with small children playing in the dirt and looking as if they'd not eaten for a long time.

As I crossed the square, I gave a few pounds to those who looked the neediest, and just as I was turning the corner to enter the bazaar area, I beheld a woman sitting with her little son, selling tissue paper. She was selling and not begging, and tissue paper was what she had in her shop. I don't know why I noticed her, but something drew all my attention toward her. I walked closer, and as I stood right in front of her, where she squatted, she looked straight up into my eyes.

Somehow, I traveled all the way into her. Her entire life story unfolded before me in a split-second glimpse. I beheld the tiny apartment of the home she'd shared with her parents, her siblings and her playing around on the dusty floor in the living room, her mother cooking in the kitchen, the smell of petrol from the streets from a mechanic shop right below their apartment. I saw her when she came of age. Beautiful, dark haired, deep brown eyes, a rounded, smiling, well-shaped face.

The images turned darker. I saw how her destiny had changed to a nightmare when she was abused by a family member, how she had become pregnant, how her own family blamed and rejected her, and how she was condemned to live on the streets with her unborn child.

I saw how later she gave birth to her son, alone in a dirty stairway, and how a neighbor in the area had felt a little mercy and helped her cut the umbilical cord, gave her a bucket to wash herself and her son, and a piece of cloth to wrap him.

How once again on the streets she was alone again, but now with a new little one. She had nothing to offer. She was entirely dependent on the mercy of others. I suddenly felt goosebumps all over my body. How cruel life can be! The man who abused her would simply have continued his life as if nothing had happened. Poor him, I thought. To be so unaware of your own doings must be a punishment in itself. Maybe the individual is not even to blame but rather a whole culture of suppressed sexuality.

I felt shocked to have seen all of that through only one deep gaze into her eyes. Seeing in this way had never opened to me before. I wanted to help her, so I asked if I could buy some tissue paper from her. She handed me one and told me to pay one Egyptian pound. I gave her a hundred and made sure no one else saw.

"*Skukran*", she said, looking a little confused when I handed her the note.

"*Shukran*", I said in return, sending her a warm smile.

I think she knew I had seen into her, because somehow there emerged, wordlessly, an understanding between us.

I felt sad not to be able to do more for either her or her son. It's not always easy to be a witness to reality as it is, to feel powerless to truly make any lasting change. I was sure there were hundreds of her with similar stories, in this city alone, not to mention in the rest of the world. I realized how fortunate I had been after all. How I had always had enough food and clothing. Always felt love and support around me. I suddenly felt guilty for having sometimes blamed my mother for not having given me a father, or for her health always being in the way of us having a normal and vital life.

Everything in this world is relative, I thought, as I once again sat down in the crowded cafe filled with shisha smoke. I ordered a mango juice and a cup of hibiscus tea while trying to calm myself down from my experience with the woman. When something like that happened to me, I always wished I could share the experience with someone, but I knew it would not really change anything even if I did. For a second, I thought about calling my mother and telling her about the incident, but I soon realized I had to grow up now, and that meant also keeping certain things and experiences to myself. Maybe one day I would tell her.

Omar, the taxi driver, was waiting for me downstairs at exactly five. I handed him the note with the address. We drove for at least an hour. The traffic was thick in the afternoon, and sometimes all the cars would stop for a few minutes, only to continue again slowly while everyone honked and yelled at each other.

Did honking really make things go faster, I asked myself? Omar, who seemed to have heard my thoughts, told me in a rather awkward English to just relax and he would get me there safely.

The Sun was already starting to set over the city, and hazy colors of orange and yellow were tinting the sky above all the buildings. An almost mystical atmosphere hung in the air. As I sat there looking out on everything taking place on the streets, I felt carried away by the sense of order abiding somehow within all the chaos. Everyone seemed to be going somewhere, taking their part in this complex web of life, creating and shaping their own destinies and entering any doors life held open for them. Every corner offered a mechanic shop, a barber shop, a food stall, or grocery store. I passed by a group of men playing chess and drinking tea on the dirty ground just next to the road. They seemed not to take the slightest notice of the all the passing cars, the sound of prayers coming from every mosque, the traffic noises blended in with the voices of the people. I felt something solemn woven into every fabric and corner of everything there. Despite all my judgement of the city and the lifestyles of its inhabitants, in that moment I felt something I could identify only as holy, infused within everything. Everyone, despite their activities, nurtured a strong belief in God. Some seemed as though they had nothing, yet beamed light from their sidelong glances. It all played itself out beautifully before me, and I felt grateful to be witnessing all of this with my own eyes and ears. As the last colors of sunset disappeared behind a tall building, we pulled over by the side of a busy road.

"Here," said Omar. "This is the address." He pointed toward a door to the left. "I got out of the car and went to look at the names on the doorbell. To my disappointment, I didn't find the name of either my aunt or her husband on the doorbell or the letter box. I decided to ring the bell of Apartment 8, where they used to live. At first, nothing. But then a voice;

"Aywa!" I assumed meant yes in Arabic.

"Do you speak English, sir? " I asked.

"Yes, very little."

"I'm looking for a couple who used to live in this apartment. Nabil and Rasha. Do you happen to know them, if they are still alive?"

"No, I'm sorry. They both passed away some years back. But I happen to know their son, who helped me buy this apartment."

"Nadim? " I asked.

"Yes," he said. "I have his number, and we can call him if

you like. Come up, and I will give it to you." He pushed a button to open the door, and once it made a little click, I pushed it open and started walking up the stairs. I was completely out of breath once I reached the eighth floor, where he had left the door open for me to come in. He greeted me kindly and told me his name was Ibrahim and that he was an old friend of Nadim.

"What brings you here?" he asked.

I wasn't sure if I should tell him why, so I just told him briefly that I was looking for some old family relatives and that I was hoping Rasha and Nabil were still alive.

Again, he told me he was sorry to bring me the sad news, but if I wanted, we could call Nadim on the phone straightaway.

I could not understand a word of what they said. It was all in Arabic. Their facial expressions, though, told me it was positive.

He put the phone down and advised me that Nadim would like to see me the following day, if five in the afternoon at Tahir Square would be possible for me, because he lived in that area.

"Sure," I said. "Just give me an address." He wrote it down and hung up.

I thanked him for all his help, and he wished me the best of luck. I left feeling very good about this next step in the direction of finding my father.

While being driven back to the hotel, I asked Omar, the driver, to pick me up the following day so that we could reach Tahir Square by five. I showed him the address, and he nodded and seemed to know the place exactly.

I imagined being a taxi driver, having to know so many places in this huge city where one can drive for hours and hours without ever seeing anything else but building after building. I paid Omar for the ride and got out of the taxi and into my hotel.

Most of the following day I felt a vague anxiety. Maybe it

was because after all these years of guessing what really happened to my father, I would most likely have some answers that very day. Maybe he was still alive somewhere, in this very city! Maybe I had already passed him or spoken to him somewhere without knowing who he was, or he, me.

After what my mother had told me about him and his relation to modern civilization, the chances seemed almost zero that he had settled in Cairo. He had lived here for several years when he was younger and built up a successful career as a photographer, back in the days before everyone could just take a picture with their cellphones. He earned a huge salary in one of the largest and most successful companies in town. He refused to shoot for companies such as Coca Cola, however. He did not agree with their business ethics and how they were buying up wells in poor parts of the world to make Coca Cola in areas where people did not even have drinking water. It takes several liters of water to make one liter of Coke. So, he simply refused to work for them despite the huge amount of money they offered. There were only a few photographers in all of Cairo then, and he was one of the best, so he had plenty of other customers. He had never been a man who cared much about money, so whenever he earned some, he easily spent it again. When my mother met him, he did not own a penny. She concluded that because he had come from a wealthy family, he simply had never really learned to handle and respect money, but I was more influenced by some of the other stories she told me about him.

For instance, he did not believe in the system of capitalism and instead chose to remain completely indifferent to its value, which resulted in him never having money and not really bothering to try to make any after the Arab revolution had turned the Egyptian economy into a catastrophe, which made his work almost impossible. I think he was living almost entirely off my mother's money when they were together, but she would always tell me that what he had given her of understanding of this world and herself was worth more than all the money in the entire world. Not to mention me. The biggest gift of her life.

Omar picked me up at exactly four, because at this time of day, the drive would take less than an hour, though it was in a neighborhood close by. He drove less aggressively than most Arabs. Something in their nature makes them feel more manly when they yell instead of talking and race instead of driving, something women can never understand.

I sat quietly, preparing myself to meet Nadim, who was actually my cousin. It just hit me that I might have more cousins. I remember my mother once mentioning that Nadim had a sister who lived in Oman or somewhere with her family. Was her name Linda? I was not certain.

Omar pulled up right in front of a fancy restaurant. He pointed to a parking place where he would wait for me.

Once inside, a waiter told me, "Mr. Nadim is busy in a meeting, but he will be here as soon as he can. What may I get you to drink, madam?"

I asked for hibiscus tea with honey, and he showed me to a table in the back of the cafe and told me this was Mr. Nadim's table. So, I supposed he came here a lot since he had his own table. I sat, feeling a little nervous and empty-handed. Five minutes passed, then ten, twenty, and soon afterward, thirty. Finally, I looked up from a sip of my hibiscus when a guy in his early fifties walked in. I knew instantly it was him. He had dark hair, a thin body, as if his body had never really become that of a man but had remained that of a boy. He greeted several people sitting around tables, and it seemed he knew everyone but advanced straight to my table, gave me his hand, and asked me what made me come and look for his parents.

Ah, I had almost forgotten that he didn't know I existed just because I knew who he was!

"I'm actually looking for your uncle Ammar," I said. "He is my father."

He stiffened a moment, then said, "I'm sorry, but I think you are mistaken. My uncle doesn't have any children."

"Do you remember a relationship he had with a Danish woman for a few years, around twenty-one years ago?"

"Yes! Salma?"

"Yes. She is my mother. Just before they broke up, she became pregnant with me, and before she even had time to tell him, he left civilization and moved to the desert somewhere. There was no way for my mother to reach him."

"Really? Is this true?" he asked with an expression on his face revealing all the surprise he must have felt. "Oh my God! You are my cousin, then!"

He stood up, came to my chair, and gave me a hug. I returned it, warmly. He was quite a warm and charming person. I already had the impression he was innately sociable.

"Didn't your mother try to tell this to my mother, at least?"

"Yes, she tried, but because of Ammar not wishing any further contact with my mother, she stopped communicating with her at all, so as not upset him."

"Yes, Ammar was a bit of an extreme character. An uncompromising fellow."

That sentence was the answer to my next question. I felt strangely heavy inside, even though I had been preparing myself for this answer for years. Still, it touched something within me. He told me that my father unfortunately had died around seven or eight years before, in the deserts of Siwa, where he was living.

"Siwa?" I asked

"An oasis in the desert close to the Libyan border. He had a farm there and farmed it on his own."

"How did he die?" I asked.

He started telling me what had happened, but I felt that talking about it made him feel a little unsettled.

"Well, nobody really knows exactly what happened, but one day he was found in the desert close to his land. Dead. But without any signs of illness or anything. It might have been a heart attack, but nobody really knew what he was even doing out there all alone. So, the most likely conclusion is that he simply felt his time to leave had arrived. I think he'd felt for a long time that his mission here on Earth had come to end, and since he was really a man of honor and pride, he would not sit around and let death take him. Rather, he welcomed it and started preparing himself for the journey. I think this is what happened. He had always been disappointed in life, and after your mother left him, he never really felt life was so easy any more. And because he never managed to become a person capable of bringing change that he had hoped to be, he must have not felt that life had anything more to offer him. But he managed to build a paradise in Siwa, where good people from all over the world would visit from time to time. And because your father was a doctor, many came to be treated by him and to heal in the peaceful surroundings. He left the property to a good friend of his called Abdulla, who had helped him run the property there and knew the land better than anyone. Your father taught him everything he knew about the world, including English, so that Abdulla was able to communicate with the people coming there from outside. And when your father left, he simply wanted Abdulla to continue running the place in his honor."

"So, he had a place there that one could visit?" I asked.

"Yes," Nadim replied. "Would you like to go? I'm sure Abdulla would love to have you there. I can give him a call and arrange something, maybe," Nadim suggested.

I agreed, but told him I needed a little time because all this new information was a little overwhelming and I needed time to process it all. He fully understood. We sat together for another hour or so. He told me more things about my father, and I told him a few things about both my mother and me.

"You know that Ammar truly loved your mother more than any other woman," Nadim told me. It felt good to hear that I after all was created out of love, even though my mother had probably told me a similar story once or twice.

"And when your mother left him, he really stopped believing in love entirely. He never wanted to be with a woman again, and ended his life living alone all these years." Poor man, I thought. Loneliness can be truly worse than hunger.

"But Ammar was strong and so full of visions," Nadim continued. "When my sister and I were children, Ammar taught us so much about life. He took us to learn diving in Sinai, taught me to paint and draw, how to sew my own clothing and make things out of wood. He always believed in me until I chose this life that I'm living now. He couldn't accept that I didn't want to follow a more natural path: one like his, in the desert with Mother Nature. So, he felt he had lost me and stopped connecting with me as much after he moved out permanently to the Oasis."

Nadim told me he had been blessed with a wife and two children now, and that they were living in a villa not far away. He had started a business some years back that was going really well, so most of the time he was not able to get out of the city. His wife, who was working as the head of a commercial company, was a modern Egyptian woman. He invited me to come to dinner and meet his family the day after, and I agreed. He wrote down the address on a piece of napkin. "Tomorrow at seven, we will be waiting for you. My wife will prepare some food." After one more goodbye hug, I thanked him for talking with me.

Back at the hotel I felt exhausted and overwhelmed from all that had happened, so I decided to call my mother and tell her about my meeting with Nadim, and what had happened with my father. I knew it would touch her profoundly. Deep within, she always carried guilt for having left, because she really loved him, though for many reasons she was unable to really accept a life with him. It had taken her years to really heal from everything, with me arriving. As a single mother. by having me she felt she had been able to retain a bit of him. So, I knew it would rile things up a little inside of her. At the moment, I needed her. I went to the reception to buy an access to Wi-Fi, logged into my Skype account, rang her, and told her about everything: the city, the bazaar, the food, the meeting with Nadim, and everything he had told me. The one thing I left out completely was Mike.

She was a little sad to hear how he had died, but told me she'd felt it inside around that time. She would meet him in her dreams a lot, and for the first time since all those years she had felt a feeling that he had truly forgiven her for leaving him and was able to understand why she had done so. More than anyone, she knew how stubborn he was. She assumed that death had been the cause of his changes. And she told me again, as often before, that my father had been a man of no compromises. For him, either you love somebody, or you don't, and if you do, why would you leave them unless you had never loved them in the first place?

That had been his final conclusion on their relationship, and so he had to cut any connection with her. She told me on the phone that after that time, she felt he was in a much better place, and finally harvested the fruits of all he had struggled through here on Earth.

"Often you plant on Earth, but you harvest in heaven, " she said on the phone.

It felt good to hear her voice that night, and before sleeping I said a little prayer of gratitude to the universe for the modern technology that made it possible for me to speak with my mother so clearly despite the thousands of kilometers between us. What an amazing invention, even though it came with a high cost, was my very last thought before sleep that night.

I decided to take it easy the next day, so stayed in bed all morning to read a book and write a bit in my diary, which was something I always indented to do but never really got around to much. I needed all my energy for the dinner today with Nadim and his family. I also wanted to look up Siwa, the place he mentioned that my father had lived all those years and built a retreat in the desert for himself as well as others to come and heal. I picked up my *Lonely Planet* handbook and started looking in the register, which pointed to several pages about Siwa: some really astonishing photos.

"Siwa is a hidden treasure, an oasis deep within the Sahara Desert of Egypt, close to the Libyan border." I kept reading:

Surrounded by sand dunes and desert mountains, it's Egypt's most isolated settlement and lies about seventy feet below sea level. It has an indigenous population of about thirty-two-thousand, who speak their own unique ancient language (Amazigh) and still practice distinct cultural traditions. They are known for their exquisite traditional embroideries, woven carpets, and traditional mud houses.

Amazigh! I suddenly remembered my mother having used the word when explaining the symbolic meaning of the necklace she had given me. That means that she must actually have been there long before she left my father. But I never remember my mother having mentioned anything about a place called Siwa. It is famous for its three large salt lakes. The water comes from having been pushed underground during the geological era when Egypt was still underwater. The oasis is home to hundreds of hot and cold mineral springs, which have been used since pharaonic times for health and vitality. The whole area sits atop the largest subterranean water reservoir in all of Egypt. Around the area, you will find lush jungles of palm trees and certain green trees that can survive with hardly any water. The region grows crops such as dates and olives, and before 1980, when they opened up a road going to a city on the coast, they were entirely self-sufficient for food, which was shared openly within the tribe. Suddenly, I remembered where I had seen the name Siwa before. I went to get my bottled water from the table in my room, and yes, just as I remembered, the label said, 'Fresh Drinking Water Straight from the Well of Siwa'. I picked up my *Lonely Planet* book again and continued reading: 'The center of Siwa is called Shali, and there you'll find the old town built on a small fortress that has stood for hundreds of years, where people carved their homes into the mountain or built a mud house as an extension of it'.

Siwa was also the home for the Oracle of Amun, who was regarded as one of the greatest Oracles of the ancient world, and was visited by Alexander the Great before continuing his Persian conquest. The legends tells that he wanted to ask the Oracle if he was a God himself. Nobody except himself knew what the answer was, but he stopped going further on his conquest and went back along the coast where he founded Alexandria.

Then there were myriads of recommendations for treatments to do there: mud baths to massages, and traditional sand baths, which sounded magical. There were colorful images of campsites right in the desert, and different suggestions of desert tours and day trips.

Wow! This place looks and sounds extraordinary, I thought to myself. I can understand from what I know about my father that he would have chosen a place like that. The image I had of him and all that I had just read and seen in the photos were in perfect harmony with one other.

I closed the book and sat quietly in bed, listening to the far sound of traffic from the streets and the dripping of water from my shower tap.

Kapital 9
Allah's Many Faces

I went into the restaurant lobby to see if I could still manage to get some late breakfast. The same waiter from the first night, who had taken me to Mike's table, assured me that everything there was possible. I only had to ask for it. So, I asked him to prepare some falafels with bread and hummus. I looked around the almost empty restaurant to find a place to sit, and I noticed a girl I had not seen before sitting at the table in the middle. At first, I couldn't help but wish that it was Mike sitting there, working on an article. I was trying hard to not let his absence get to me the past days, but in that moment, I felt a cloud of longing coming towards me. I took a deep breath, and turned my attention back to the present moment.

From a distance I estimated her to be around my age, or slightly older. She looked European in a pair of jeans and a white t-shirt, and from a distance I felt she was somehow a little lonely. Something in my gut told me to walk over and introduce myself. I went to sit by a table nearby, to wait for my food, and maybe send a few messages on my phone. So many people had been writing me, asking how it was going, if I had arrived safely, if I had found my father yet, and a message from my friend Sophie telling me that Denmark had been rainy and cold. All these lovely messages and people caring for me, and then I felt I couldn't really be bothered answering. I thought a little about it and concluded that maybe it was not so much that I could not be bothered. Responding would somehow split my reality in two, having to be both here and there at the same time. Somehow it would take me away from the intensity of the here and now. And with all these messages, Denmark seemed so close by, and my adventure less adventurous. Maybe this is what happens when people get stressed in the modern world, when life demands them to be in a hundred places at the same time. Feeling themselves neither really here nor really there, they end up becoming a fraction of themselves, constantly floating between worlds and never really arriving fully in any of them. I can answer those messages later, I thought, and put the phone away in my pocket. I should rather try to make a conversation with the woman sitting at the table beside me, but what could I ask her? She appeared to be concentrating on a book or a map, I couldn't really see clearly.

"I haven't seen you around here before. Did you just arrive?" I asked.

She turned around, looked at me with a bit of nervousness in her eyes, then told me she had been in Cairo for two weeks, staying at a different hotel that she had not liked, something about bad hygiene. To judge from the hand sanitizer on the table in front of her, I think this meant a lot to her, so she had been recommended to this hotel for its decent price and Western standards.

"So, you like it here better?" I asked.

She told me how amazing this place was compared to the other, how friendly the staff were, and how welcome Muhammad had made her feel from the first moment. Her accent told me she was more American than European, and from her enthusiasm about having somebody to talk to. I guess my intuition that she felt a little lonely proved accurate.

"I'm from Ohio," she told me. "And where are you from?"

I told her my name and nationality, and she shared that her name was Sally. Because the weather was unbelievably hot that day, it was too exhausting to leave the hotel. So, she had planned to go and watch a movie in a shopping mall about a twenty-minute drive away, and she asked me to join her. Because I didn't have any other plans, and it was nice to take my mind off my quest for my father, I agreed to come along.

In the taxi, she told me she was studying something at university called Studies of the Middle East, and that she had started out studying religion but became so taken with the Middle East and Islam that she switched majors. Actually, she had been interested in the Middle East and Islam since childhood, when a woman from Syria her family had employed helped around the house. The Syrian woman told Sally stories of old tales from the Arab world, great stories from times of peace and harmony, where kings had once ruled with care and justice for all the people. That was before men started fighting each other and destroying themselves and one another because of oil, power, and money. This is what it often comes down to in the end: a disregard for life and for the health of Mother Nature. She continued telling me about how she had been brought up in the countryside, outside the city, by a very conservative father and an absent mother. Her father's greatest fear for his only daughter was that she had chosen a career to understand and work with immigrants. He never really paid attention to the woman who kept his house clean for twenty years, paid her very little, and made her feel that he was doing her a huge favor by letting her work for him. He told her she should not even really be in the country, which did not belong to her. But this woman was strong and warmhearted. She accepted her destiny and never stopped believing that Allah was taking care of her. She cleaned houses for twenty years, without ever complaining or seeming unsatisfied with her reality.

Back then, it made Sally wonder about all these people she knew who had all the privileges in the world and yet were never satisfied at all. Maybe less is more, maybe all these desires of a modern life are actually making us more unhappy and more disconnected. Look at this woman who had nothing, who lost both her sons and her husband in the war, who had been forced to leave her country only to come here and live with her sister, who ended up getting a permit to stay, only to clean other people's dirt every day for twenty years, earning only enough to pay for the rent of a one-room apartment and food. And still she believed in God, and that life was good and beautiful. While cleaning she would often sing old Arabic songs of lost times, and sometimes when she thought nobody was looking, she would dance around a little and pretend the vacuum cleaner was her dance partner.

Sally was taken by the harmony and peace of this woman, and later on she realized she wanted to study their culture to better understand them, so she could eventually work with them. Sally had realized what true happiness is, only because of the grace of the cleaning woman. Not long after getting involved in their culture, Sally realized that not all people from that part of the world enjoyed the same peaceful relation to Allah, and when there was a school shooting that killed five kids when a young extremist who believed that what he had done was in the name of Allah, she wondered if they were talking about the same Allah. But still, she insisted on studying the paradoxes of their culture. She wanted to know and understand more, and now she was here in Cairo, taking an Arabic language course before working as part of her studies, at a social project for homeless people in a poor Cairo neighborhood.

I was enjoying her stories and her company, even though she spoke for a long time. She told me all of this after I just barely mentioned my name. Actually, though, it felt good for once not always having to tell my own story, but rather to listen to the concerns of someone else. There are so many stories out there. There are the stories that we tell, and then there are the stories that tell us, and every human being has their own unique life story that belongs only to them.

We got out of the taxi and found ourselves in front of a huge mall. "Just like in America," Sally commented.

And yes, she was right. Inside there were mostly only American chain shops, except for a Swedish H&M and a Spanish Zara. Everything else was McDonalds, KFC, Starbucks, you name it. It was like stepping into another world, and because the whole mall was nicely air-conditioned, we forgot for a while we were even in Egypt. The place was full of young people shopping, going on dates, having their hair done, or waiting for their food to be served.

This is where the rich would spend their afternoons, escaping the heat and the chaos outside, filling in the void we all have inside with new clothing and countless other items. That afternoon we watched one of the worst romantic Hollywood movies I had ever seen. But I didn't mind; it felt like the perfect escape from reality.

Upon returning back to the hotel, while lying in bed that night waiting for sleep to arrive, I found myself again sending Mike a longing thought. How lovely it could be to have him here next to me, or at least to have gotten to spend some more time together. Strange, that I felt so connected to somebody I had only known for such a brief time.

Chapter 10
Sunsets on Prescription

Nadim's apartment was modern and light, located on a rooftop in a busy part of the area. Because it was perched atop the ten-story building, however, I felt almost completely above all the noise and chaos below.

His wife, Lara, greeted me at the entrance, welcoming me and apologizing for her husband being busy on the phone with an important business call. She assured me he would join us soon.

He seemed like a busy man, I thought, but as if she had read my mind, she continued, saying, "well, this is almost always the case, but he cancelled several meetings to be here with you tonight."

She showed me inside, and made me a cold drink of lemon, mint, and about a ton of sugar, as is the tradition here. Then she led me to the rooftop to sit and enjoy the view over the city while she prepared the rest of the food.

She told me a little apologetically that both children were out, so I would have to meet them another time. They were seventeen and nineteen, so not so easy to keep at home any more. I nodded to show that I fully understood and was pleased with the situation just as it was.

She was a short and warm woman with a friendly smile, and seemed to exude positive energy. As I sat there overlooking the city, above all the noise but still not far away from it, I again felt like soon getting out of the city. I started to feel a little confined by everything: all these man-made buildings, the traffic, the shops, the roads and street lights, the lack of peace and quiet. All were really starting to get to me. Some landscapes inspiring reflection and contemplation would do good to my soul. I had tried to meditate a few times in my room, but shortly after had given up with all the constant distractions from outside.

I wasn't sure I was quite ready to go to this Oasis of Siwa yet. Maybe the time was not ripe. Everything had gone so quickly since I arrived, and so much had happened in less than a week. Maybe I should ask Nadim where would be a nice place to go for a few days.

We sat around the table, all three of us, eating the food Lara had prepared. First was rice, prepared in an Arabic manner where you first fry it in oil before you cook it, so the texture changes. Next, some lady fingers with spices and a green salad. The food indicated they were living healthily and not eating fast food like the rest of the city. Nadim told me he'd suffered stomach problems when he was younger, and spent entire periods only in bed because of the pain. He later changed his life entirely, training his body every morning with martial arts and tai chi, eating only organic food, and meditating to foster positive thoughts. And this had all been because of his uncle, my father.

"Ammar taught me everything he knew about the body and how to heal it," he said. "Did you know that he was trained as a medical doctor?"

I nodded in confirmation.

"He didn't believe so much in Western medicine when he began working as a doctor. After he finished medical school, he soon realized that he didn't have any tools to really heal people. He began feeling utterly helpless seeing people come to his office only to leave with some pills that could maybe treat the symptom but never the cause. He knew that in many causes the pills would bring on new problems, which would call for new pills. So, he saw his patients getting worse and worse and often dying from side effects of their medications rather than the illness they were being treated for." Nadim's face had grown serious.

"As you know, your father was a man of no compromises, so he stopped working as a doctor and began studying holistic medicine. When he combined his knowledge of both worlds, he really managed to gain a good overall understanding of what good health really means. He started treating people differently then. When anyone came to see him for some help, he would not only look at their physical health but also their psychological condition. He would ask what they were doing in their lives, whether they were happy or not. If they were smokers, he would make them break all their cigarettes before he let them leave the office, telling them it was truly for the best. Often, he would send them home with some herbs, some general changes in diet, some exercises to perform every morning before starting the day, and some new activities they had to perform. He would prescribe things such as going to watch a sunset or sunrise every day, taking a swim at a lake, or going for a walk at night under the stars. 'Through connecting with Mother Nature, you connect to your very self,' he would always tell his patients. He believed that many illnesses come from certain patterns in the brain created from routine. For example, a condition such as Alzheimer's can result from the brain having repeated the same thought over and over until the true capacity of the brain to think a new thought and see new possibilities has become so small that the mind is no longer able to connect with and relate any more to a larger picture, or to their origin of life.

"It might sound strange," said Nadim, "but often I really believed he was onto something. Many times, he would tell his patients to go find a place of grass or sand and put their bare feet on the Earth, and that by doing so they would connect to the electromagnetic forces of the Earth, which has incredible healing capacities that tune in to the electromagnetic forces of the body. Sometimes he would tell people to encircle their bed with a wire and extend it all the way out the window and plug it into the Earth so they would be connected to the planet all through their sleep.

"Sadly, though, Ammar quickly discovered that many of his patients preferred to just take a pill rather than having to perform some activity themselves. Some, he realized, had grown so much into the identity of their illnesses that they couldn't even know who they were without it. Ammar was not the most patient man when it came to his patients, so if they didn't prove to him quickly that they were willing to follow some of his advice and start making some changes, he would refuse to see them a second time."

I remember my mother having said something similar in relation to my father and her health issues. We sat for a while longer on the rooftop, and Nadim told me more stories about my father. I listened eagerly, taking in every word as compensation for what I would never get to experience myself. Nadim told me he had a cousin who was also my cousin, of course. The cousin lived in Cairo as well, but often was away working for long periods on some oil drilling projects. He had a wife and one child, and maybe I could meet him at some point when he was back in the city again.

Nadim and Lara were really lovely people, and both spoke English fluently, which made the conversation smooth and free of any misunderstandings. I left their flat that evening with a warm feeling of having extended my family wonderfully. Even with my father no longer here, he would still remain alive through the people who had known and loved him. Maybe in this way we get to live a lot longer, I thought to myself on my way back in the taxi.

Chapter 11
Burkinis and Landfills

Sally was waiting at the reception desk to ask for some clean towels or something when I was about to go out to get some lunch the next day.

"Where are you going?" she asked.

I told her I wanted to go back to the *shisha* restaurant I had become somehow familiar with, and she decided to join me even before I was able to invite her along. But I didn't mind. I found her company to be a good distraction from my own constant thoughts, and she seemed happy to have somebody to talk with. She told me her language lesson had been cancelled that day because her teacher was down with the flu. And since the Coronavirus pandemic, the whole world had become terrified to catch just an ordinary flu. We walked down the same streets I had walked a few times now, passed by the bazaar where Sally wanted to do some shopping, and went into several shops and tried on traditional Egyptian clothing. Sally even tried on a burka. I didn't know if it was inappropriate, but the owner of the shop seemed to find it quite entertaining, only to be a bit disappointed when we ended up not actually buying anything.

"It's too early for me on my journey to do a lot of shopping," I told Sally. "Otherwise my backpack will be so heavy I will end up not being able to move."

She agreed. She had the same thought, but because she didn't plan on really traveling much because of her language course and the volunteer program, she ended up buying a few cashmere shawls and a nice cotton dress. Good for her, with a dress and not these warm jeans, I thought to myself.

It was quite pleasant to just be a tourist for a while. Eating out in restaurants, taking taxis around town, not having to worry too much about money, because everything was far cheaper than at home. All these things I had never really done before. We never had enough money to eat out a lot, my mother and I, and the price of a taxi in Denmark is about the cost of a week of good food there, so that also wasn't really a thing in my childhood. Sally and I ended up back at the same cafe, where I brought some fresh watermelon juice and a pancake with dates and honey inside, while Sally insisted on buying the shisha pipe and at least trying it once while we were there, as a part of the experience. It resulted in both of us coughing horribly for a while and agreeing that we had tried enough for a whole lifetime.

I started to feel I had really had enough of the city: all the pollution, people, cars, and shops everywhere. Maybe my father had actually been right when he told Nadim he had to leave the city in order to truly heal. I looked in my *Lonely Planet* book for options and places to go, but because I wasn't really ready to go to Siwa yet, and many other tourist attractions seemed possible to experience only in groups, I decided to spend a few days on the coast.

Nadim owned a villa there and had offered me an opportunity to go and vacation there for a few days. The house just stood empty, and they couldn't find any time to go there in the near future, with him being busy with his company. I decided to ask Sally to come along because I knew she didn't have classes on weekends. She did not have any other friends here other than me, apart from a few Turkish immigrants from her language class who mainly spoke Turkish to each other. She agreed to come along. Nadim even arranged with his driver to take us all the way, even though the drive was several hours.

"It would really be my pleasure to know you will stay there for a few days and make the house a little less lonely," he assured me when I tried to tell him I didn't know if I could accept this generous offer. So, I ended up thanking him profusely, and he told me he would even send somebody there to make sure we had everything we needed in the house. Two days later I checked out of the hotel. Sally kept her room because she would be back again in two days. I said goodbye to Muhammad and the friendly waiter in the restaurant who always made sure I got the food I desired. I thanked everyone, and we were now on our way out of Cairo.

It took several hours just to get out of the city, and the traffic was draining as usual. I couldn't wait to feel some fresher air.

The season had just started on the coast, and most people were still not on vacation, so it wouldn't be too crowded yet. We finally made it to the outskirts of the city and crossed the Nile. I felt so excited to finally see her in real life in all her beauty. In Egypt, they always refer to her as a woman, because she is the source that sustains and makes all life fertile. She looked stunning in her blue, glittering colors, with her waters flooding all her banks and making agriculture possible. People grew everything there, and vast areas of farmland bordered both banks. Everything: greens, grains and fruits flourished. Farm animals grazed in green pastures. It was lovely to see some green again, I thought to myself. Unfortunately, the Nile was not as clean as it formerly had been. Somebody in Cairo told me she was so polluted by now that it took more energy to filter her water and make it drinkable than it would be to just use saltwater from the ocean.

I remembered something about a mass murder in Sudan. Tons of bodies had been dumped into the water. The decomposing bodies apparently contributed to the rise of bacteria, which made it dangerous even to swim. Many grew sick from parasites or bacteria burrowing through the skin all the way into their intestines. There are also environmental chemicals and pesticides they had started using in agriculture to enhance their yields and kill off unwanted insects. Without knowing so, however, these chemicals might end up killing humans as well as insects.

Still, though, this was the Nile, the longest river in the whole world. Ancient Egypt would have never even existed without her. And because Egypt is among one of the driest countries on Earth, with rainfall extremely rare, she has been the only source of water. Agriculture all along her banks was what brought food to the people when huge rainfalls in Ethiopia made water levels rise. When they sank again, they would leave the fields on the banks muddy and perfect for growing. She was the center of life then, and the ancient Egyptians knew her value and often prayed and presented offerings to her, the source of all life.

Traveling on the Nile was the easiest and most rapid way to go anywhere, and for centuries she was the central trade route. Often in our modern lives we completely forget where things actually come from. We just turn on the tap in our apartment, flush the toilet, and never even think where that water comes from or where it will go. Many modern children think that food comes from the supermarket and not from the Earth, because it is the only place they have ever seen it. So sad did I feel inside, that I made a promise if I ever had children, I would teach them to garden just like my grandfather had once taught me.

Half an hour's drive further out, we started to reach some

desert-looking landscapes. We both felt happy to leave the city and see something else, but just as we left the last outskirts of the city, the entire area turned into a landfill, a place where trash is dumped because nobody knows how to get rid of the huge mountains of debris produced by modern living. We drove for kilometers and kilometers with only trash along both sides of the road, nothing but plastic and the wind constantly playing with it and spreading it to even larger areas. This is the price nature pays for our consumerism. If this continues, one day the entire globe might be covered in plastic, I thought to myself, feeling a little hopeless.

Sally, who noticed my depressed mood, tried to cheer me up with some biscuits and apple juice she'd brought along. The landfills did eventually come to an end, and we were driving in the desert now, with a few trees and bushes here and there the only vegetation. It was not soft desert sand as I had imagined, but harder and more condensed, light-colored soil. We had been driving for a few hours when I started to notice some clouds in the sky.

"That means we are getting close to the coast," I told Sally.

The air also started to feel more humid and fresher, with a soft smell of iodine blown on the wind.

Nadim had warned me to be careful when swimming. "You have no idea how unpredictable the waters can be here. Many people end up drowning there every summer because they simply don't respect the power of the ocean," he told me.

I believed him because the west coast of Denmark can be pretty wild at times also. After reaching the coast, we drove for another hour or so down along the waterfront, heading west before finally stopping at a huge guarded entrance to a gated community.

'Marina Entrance 7' announced a huge blue electric sign. I supposed we had already passed the other six entrances, so I concluded that it had to be a huge place. Our driver clearly knew the people at the entrance, and they let us in without having to show any ID or papers. We drove down a few streets and stopped in front of a large, white, Greek-looking villa.

"It is here," he said, helping us out of the car with our bags and into the house. He promised to be back and pick up Sally in two days.

It was a lovely, light, and modern house with windows facing north, so one could look straight to the waterfront and out into the wide-open arms of the ocean. We each had a room upstairs, and Sally seemed to be overly pleased with the standard of hygiene she had not managed to find in Cairo, at least not at her first hotel. Everything seemed to have been prepared for our arrival, and a house maid was in the kitchen preparing some dinner for us.

Nadim must be worth a fortune, I thought, feeling a little uncomfortable with all this luxury, to which I was unaccustomed. How could I accept all of this without giving anything in return? I knew Nadim would never accept any money from me. It helped a little to see how comfortable it made Sally. She clearly came from a different standard of living than myself and was accustomed to having a cleaning lady and a cook in the house.

Because it was already getting dark, we decided to take a walk down to the beach. Twilight is usually around six there, unlike in the north, where you have light-filled summer evenings. The waves looked refreshing, and there were a few surfers trying to catch the last rides before sunset forced them back on land. We decided to take a swim first thing in the morning.

There were a few bars starting to open up along the

beachfront, and some pop music mixed with the sound of the waves. This was really a place for the wealthy to come and enjoy life. We went back and enjoyed some delicious seafood cooked by the housemaid.

"Freshly caught this morning," she told us, and we enjoyed a solid meal. All this luxury, I had to admit, I was starting to enjoy, even though it felt somehow against my nature. It was good to be away from the city at least, and good to have Sally there with me, even though we actually hardly knew each other. We spent a nice weekend there swimming, eating well, and taking every opportunity to sleep in without being woken up at four by the first morning prayers from the mosque.

The wealthy here clearly had a more relaxed and casual relationship to Allah, despite many still following certain rules. When swimming in the ocean, they wore a whole swimsuit, or a *burkini*, as they called them.

Chapter 12
New Landscapes

Sally was just leaving with Nadim's driver. We hugged each other goodbye and wished each other a good and healthy life, both knowing we would possibly never see each other again. I decided to stay another night until I could get a local bus from there to a little further down the coast, and then transfer to another shuttle bus to the Oasis of Siwa. In total it was a journey of eight or nine hours from where I was now, and if I got on an early morning bus the next day, I could make it to Siwa before sunset.

I looked for a place to sleep in the center because I was arriving late and found a place called Paradise Lodge, run by a fellow called Josef, who according to *Lonely Planet*, was a very good cook. I wrote down the address of the hotel so I could ask for directions as soon as I arrived.

The next morning, I found myself on a bumpy local bus packed with workers going to the city. Because I was the only woman on board, I quickly became the center of attention. Everywhere I looked, eyes were staring straight at me, and all the attention made me feel a little insecure. I made sure my shawl was tightly wrapped around me so that not one inch of skin would be revealed.

I don't think they had ever seen a Western woman on this kind of bus. Usually, tourists take a luxury, overnight, air-conditioned shuttle bus from Cairo, spend all night sleeping on a double seat, and wake up in Siwa feeling completely fresh and rested. This would surely not be the case here. I looked around the bus, which was so old that the glass was broken in some of the windows. I don't think most of them could even close any more, but it was nice to have the fresh air coming in. I went to the back of the bus to sit next to a guy wearing a nice bright green turban. He looked at me with a friendly smile, and I felt safe enough to choose the empty seat on his left.

The workers on the bus were clearly simple people, Bedouins who used to work and live in the desert, but now were forced to work in the cities to make their livings. They used to be nomads, living in tribes or clans in the desert, in regions stretching from North Africa and into the Middle East. The word Bedouin actually means "desert dweller" in Arabic, and they have a culture of herding camels and goats. Many today have abandoned their traditions and have gone into the cities, drawn by urban lifestyles, but still a few have kept their traditions alive with song, dance, poetry, and cooking. They used to be an extremely peaceful population, living close with nature, sleeping outside under the open sky, knowing how to survive under difficult and simple conditions, but they, along with the rest of the world, began changing.

Only one man on the bus asked for my nationality by saying, "country which"? The rest left me alone to sit and look out at the passing landscape.

The roads were horrible, full of bumps and cracks, and every time I found a good position to sit in, the bus would go a little too fast and the whole vehicle would jump half a meter in the air, with me, rather awkwardly, needing to readjust my body to another position. The bus driver clearly did not seem to have a driver's license, or maybe the bus didn't have a speedometer to tell him how fast it was safe to drive. All part of the experience,

I thought, for it reminded me of my aunt's stories about her trips through India in local trains, sitting in the open doors smoking cigarettes while the train was chugging along, and the world outside passing by while she enjoyed her moment of absolute freedom.

I got off the bus in a place called Matrouh, a large city further along the coast. It was the closest town to Siwa. There were still another few hours of travel before reaching Siwa, and I had to wait an hour for my next bus, just enough time to buy some street falafels and some fried eggplants with baba ganoush for lunch. I felt as if I were living like a local. People always warned me about eating anything from the streets, terrified of foreign bacteria and viruses, but I often found that the food was both fresher and tastier where the locals ate. Because I didn't have a lot of money, it felt good to just grab something from these open food stalls. One day in Cairo, though, I caught a stomach flu and ended up running to the bathroom the whole night. Luckily, it all resolved itself by the next day, and after that I felt as if my stomach was even stronger than before.

The roads were even worse along the next stretch, and sometimes the whole bus had to veer off-road because the desert itself was better than the road. We had to drive extremely slowly and make a few stops along the way, checking if the wheel on the engine was okay.

The landscape started changing, flat desert becoming undulant and then rising into mountainous formations: flat, strange-looking mountains with layers of variously colored rocks. I couldn't remember ever having seen anything like it: the rainbow-colored strata of rocks and minerals, the places where minerals were less heavy than in others, so that the wind had carved remarkable notches inside the mountains, leaving behind a sculpture formed and perfected over millennia by the formless artistry of wind and rain. Now these forms stood strong and solid, for a geological instant displaying their present beauteous forms.

I remembered my mother having always told me that nature is truly the greatest artist, and in that moment I couldn't agree more. The place must really be a geologist's and anthropologist's paradise, I thought. The entire panorama bore witness to eons of evolution, revealing here how these forms had been formed, flowing into their present formations.

I remembered having read in a geology book back in high school that a lot of the finest, small-grained sand you can find is sculpted from the shells of living beings from the ocean, crushed by waves and wind over and over for eons and eons, almost erased, but forming the most perfectly soft beach for beings to enjoy. It made me feel awed to know this entire world is alive and has a soul.

Deeply embedded within the beauty of the landscape and my own thoughts, I noticed a sign saying 'Siwa 10 Km'. An explosion of butterflies fluttered in my belly. After all these years and all this time, I was going to see the place where my father had lived. Of course, I would have wished to meet him there and to really get to know him, and more of those sides of myself that had come from him and his nature and his nurturing culture.

So often we think we don't need each other to know ourselves, which is not really true. It is through each other, through relationships, that we know ourselves. Deep inside all of us is an innate longing to know ourselves and from where we have come. Not everyone, though, dares to enter upon this path of self-discovery, for often it is full of not only flowers, but also thorns.

For the next few kilometers, the road turned into a dust road, and soon we were on the final approach leading into the Center of Shali as the last colors of the Sun were fading in the sky above.

The bus stopped at what looked like the main square, with a few cafes and some food markets. I got up, put my backpack on, and left the bus. I then stood for a while outside, not knowing where to go and who to ask. Because the light was already starting to dim, I did not have so much time to orient myself before it grew dark.

The place looked smaller than I had imagined. The roads were dirt, and I remembered having read in my *Lonely Planet* guide that the first road out of Siwa had been built in the 1980s. Before that, they were an enclosed, self-sufficient civilization. The whole scene looked simple and natural. The colors of the mud buildings constructed from the muddy soil, and the desert sand, made the dwellings seem both apart from and part of their surroundings: extensions of nature rather than some foreign, awkward skyscraper.

I wanted to have a proper look around, but first I had to find a place for the night. A few men were sitting and talking around a table at a cafe down the road from the bus stop, so I decided to go and ask them where to find Paradise Lodge. They all knew Yousef and his hotel, and instead of telling me where to find it, they called him to pick me up, and in less than twenty minutes I found myself happily installed in a simple mud house, waiting while Yousef prepared dinner for me.

Everybody seemed to know each other there, and while walking back with Yousef to his hotel, everyone greeted him and several people stopped to ask him something. Probably they were all related in family, I thought to myself, and remembered having read that there used to only be a few tribes out here. Yousef fed me some lovely food cooked on a bonfire, which added a nice smoked flavor, and I concluded that the review in *Lonely Planet* was trustworthy.

Afterwards, I went straight to my room and almost passed out on the bed. My legs were sore and tired from sitting on the bumpy bus all day, and my senses needed rest from all the images of changing landscapes. That night I slept the deepest ever, until I was awakened by a strange and unusual dream.

I found myself in a large house somewhere. I heard a loud bump from outside. I went out on a porch to see what it was. Right in front of me, I saw the Sun hitting the Earth, and everything bursting into flames. The flames spread rapidly, so I wanted to escape, and I turned around only to realize the flames had spread everywhere. The whole Earth was in flames, and I realized that soon I would die. Smoke and flames moved closer and closer, and with the knowledge that I would soon be swallowed in flames, I just stood there on the porch, awaiting my own death, yet feeling strangely peaceful.

I woke up covered with sweat, as if my waking body had actually been subjected to the heat from the dream flames.

Would the Sun one day hit Earth? I remembered once having read that Earth's rotation slowly moves closer and closer to the Sun. Surely, I had dreamt about dying before, but this time it seemed so clear. Yet I put up no fight nor felt the slightest hint of fear. Strange, I guessed I would have to consult with one of my mother's dream-interpreting friends when I got home. I took a little time to write down the details of the dream in my diary so I would not forget before I had time to ask somebody about it.

Now with the morning light having come, I could really take in the details of my room. The walls were made from light-colored mud mixed with something like straw, and the texture was rough and natural, with a piece of wall cracked around the corners. On the floor laid a lovely woven blanket of red and white, with animal figures woven into the middle and some fridges on the side. It was one of the traditional local carpets I had read about in my guidebook. There was only a small window looking out into the hotel garden, a lush little park of date palms and olive trees. It seemed as though the dates were plump and ready to eat, for a few had already fallen on the ground. I decided to go and eat some as soon as I showered.

Yousef made me some pancakes with banana and dates for breakfast, and a cup of strong Arabic coffee full of sugar. The dates were of course from his own garden, he told me, and the bananas from his uncle's farm on the coast. He'd managed to pick up English quite well by having spent a lot of time with the tourists, and because most people here spoke only Arabic or Amazigh (the local Berber tongue), I could always come to him and ask him things.

I hadn't asked him yet if he had known my father, but because everyone seemed to know each other, he definitely would have. I somehow felt like remaining anonymous a little longer, at least for this first day. I wanted just to go around and explore a little on my own. I packed a little bag and left the hotel with the intention of going to look at the old part of town. I walked through the little Center, which was still slowly waking up. Yousef had told me that most places would be closed until midday because it was Friday, when everyone goes to the mosque for morning prayers. Friday is their Sunday here, and as I walked through the little street of the cafe from last night, all I could hear were loud prayers and chants cried out from all sides. I supposed people out here were really religious, and I just realized I had not seen a single woman on the streets yet or in any of the shops. Sad,

I thought. I would have liked to see the faces of these local women. I was sure they would look stunning in all their hidden beauty. A few young boys, not more than seven or eight, passed me on their motorcycles, and I was shocked to see that their parents were letting them drive at such a young age. That would be unthinkable in Denmark and would result in large fines. I guessed such rules and bureaucracy were nonexistent out here. Later I learned that actually, quite a few accidents happened around there because of these young drivers, and often the people involved would end up losing one of their limbs or gaining a permanent head injury, or something else devastating to their quality of life.

A few people looked at me as if they had never seen a woman, or a white woman before, and even with my body completely covered up and a shawl wrapped around my hair, I didn't manage to escape the fact that I was a foreigner. Everyone, though, seemed to be kind and friendly, and many greeted me with '*as-salam alaykom*', meaning 'hello', or a '*hamdullah*', meaning something like 'I thank God for his blessings'.

The Bedouins wore traditional clothing: long cotton dresses and turbans wrapped around their heads as protection against the Sun. All was woven of mellow colors somehow melting into the tints of the desert all around. Only a few jeeps and motorcycles lined the streets, but most people used donkeys to transport themselves and their crops around. With a whole trolley attached to the donkey's back, they could transport a whole family and a large load of groceries. I couldn't help but feel a little sorry for the donkeys. What a completely different world out here! I felt as if I had gone to sleep and suddenly awakened in another century, perhaps on an entirely different planet. Maybe this is what my dream had tried to tell me: that I had died in flames and had now risen to a new and different reality. I looked around the remains of the old city, mostly ruins of houses once built straight into the mountains, carved into them, and I imagined how it must have felt living there then and what simple and difficult lives the people must have lived.

The whole place was impressive, and at the top of the fortress stood an ancient mosque. I took some time to look around the whole area and to really get a feeling of the atmosphere and spirit of the place.

After my brief sightseeing around the Center, I went to sit at the cafe, where I'd asked for directions the night before. When I arrived there, almost all tables were occupied, and it seemed to be an immensely popular place for both locals and tourists.

A group of what looked like upper-class people from Cairo had pushed a few tables together and were enjoying their breakfast while speaking and laughing loudly. A few Bedouins were sitting around another table drinking tea, smoking cigarettes, and speaking in a language that didn't sound like Arabic. Must be the local Amazigh, I thought to myself. It sounded softer than Arabic and had more of a rhythm to it. I ordered some tea and a fresh watermelon juice, and sat down by the last available table in a corner of the cafe. One of the local people drinking tea at another table came up to me. He told me his name was Ismael and that his job was to take people on trips into the desert.

"Let me know if you need a guide or something," he said with a strange English accent I hadn´t heard previously.

I told him that I usually preferred to explore on my own, but maybe at some point later I might really need him. He gave me his card and told me he would be at my service any time.

Despite the accent, I noticed he spoke English quite well for a Bedouin, so he told me his wife is an American woman, Samantha, and together they were running a little shop in Alexandria, selling soaps and natural groceries here from Siwa. She had been brought up in New York, he told me, but with a father originally from Alexandria, she always felt Egyptian at heart, and as soon as she finished university, she came here to visit some family. That is when they met and fell in love.

Sometimes destiny can seem so coincidental, as if random events had led to their meeting, which entirely changed her path. The longer I lived, the surer I became aware of forces greater than ourselves. I knew they led us to the people we are ready for and the challenges we must confront on our path to know ourselves and the world around us.

"I'm sure my wife would love to meet you," he said. "Sometimes she misses having somebody to really speak English with. Even though she is teaching me, I am still only learning," he added. "Maybe I can invite you to our home in the afternoon?"

I accepted the invitation. He seemed to be a kind, gentle fellow, and his invitation sounded like a good opportunity to get to know some people living here. We agreed on him picking me up the same afternoon at four, outside the cafe.

I went back to Yousef's place to rest for a few hours, showered, and changed into some fresh clothing. I still had not even told anybody there why I had actually come, or asked them anything about my father.

Ismael picked me up as planned, drove me to the outskirts of the village, and took me to a shady house of stone and concrete, not like the traditional buildings. More and more, people wanted to build and live like those in the cities. Instead of building from the mud, salt, and clay they had used for centuries, they demanded cement and bricks.

"This is my family home," Ismael told me before we entered.

I just realized that of course this is how it is here. You live with your entire family, and when I entered, I found his mother, father, and younger brother living under the same roof as Ismael and his Samantha. They were all warmhearted and seemed glad to have me as their dinner guest, especially Samantha.

At first, I felt a little shocked to discover she was completely covered in a black burka. All I could see was her eyes. Because I had not yet on my journey spoken to many Muslim women, it took a while to adjust to the lack of facial expressions. I had to rely only on gestures and the light of the eyes, not from the entire face as I was used to. It reminded me of those times during the Corona outbreak where the whole world was wearing masks. It had been really horrible and created so much fear and distance amongst everyone.

I soon realized that Samantha was a quiet Western woman inside, just like myself.

She told me the story of how she had grown up in the middle of New York city, raised by an American mother and an Egyptian father. She had been brought up as a Muslim, but never a strict one like those here. After high school she decided to study economics because her father was a well-known banker. Because he always made good money to provide for the family, Samantha reasoned that business was the recipe for a good life. So, she went through a few years of business school before realizing that doing so was definitely not her path.

Every day she had become more and more sad and depressed about life, and the more she learned about economics and growth, the worse she felt.

"This whole system of capitalism is really unhealthy and

unsustainable, only making the rich richer and the poor poorer. The more you understand about money, the more you realize that it is an illusion, or more precisely a value we have all agreed on that is actually not based on anything real," she said. "Did you know that the wealthiest one percent of the world's population now owns more than half of the world's wealth? And why is it that we live in a world where a lawyer gets paid ten times more than a farmer? Without the farmer, the lawyer would have nothing to eat."

I nodded to confirm that I was familiar with this inequality, and I remembered many complaints from my mother about these matters and all her attempts to write papers on these topics and try to have them published somewhere, without much success.

"And the people studying these things start only caring about materialistic things, and one day you wake up within the frame of a city like New York and realize how far you have moved away from God and anything natural," she said with a sigh. "Even the air and humidity of the city started making me sick and unable to breathe," she continued. "And with a system that always prioritizes quantity over quality, beauty along with biodiversity and many animals today are extremely endangered. How can we, as humanity, possible progress from a declining system as such?" she asked out loud.

She told me that because of her Muslim upbringing, she had always felt life as larger and more beautiful than what reality presented to her. That experience planted some seeds inside. So, when she really admitted to herself what the city was doing to her, she instantly quit her studies and got on a plane to stay with some family in Alexandria. Not long after arriving there, she met Ismael, who was just a simple Bedouin coming into Alexandria to sell his groceries. They fell in love.

A few months later, she married him. Something unthinkable, for a woman such as herself to marry a simple Bedouin from the desert who had no position, no fortune in money or property, with all he could offer her being the living he eked out from a small olive grove and the income of a few desert tours for tourists.

Nothing in her entire life had ever felt righter. In the end her family accepted her decision and helped her open up a shop in Alexandria so they could hire somebody there to sell their things to make enough money to sustain their living. Then she married Ismael, knowing she would have to live a life like a local Bedouin woman out in the desert. She gave up all her American clothing, makeup, and self-image in exchange for a burka and a profession as a wife living at home. In other words, she chose to become nobody in the eyes of society.

Her life was hidden away in a far and isolated corner of the world, in a dwelling housing with only her husband and his family. There, she slowly dissolved her own personal history and created a completely different reality. She spoke Arabic already and was now studying Amazigh, an essential skill for blending in with the community of local women. She wanted that, needed that.

The world of the intellect in New York, and all the illusions of society had started to make her spirit wither. She felt far away from Allah. But out in the desert she could be herself. She could breathe again, not only because the desert air is some of the cleanest on Earth, but because she escaped the labyrinth of constant self-identification and could now simply rest her being in the arms of Mother Nature.

"So, are you happy now?" I dared to ask her.

She told me that life always has its challenges everywhere,

and that quite frankly it was not easy for a woman with a Western mind to go and live a simple life with simple people, but every day when the Sun rises over the desert, and every night after setting again, the most amazing night sky blossoms above. It is then that she feels the closest to Allah and all of creation. Everything else becomes small and insignificant while slowly, over time, her own small personal desires begin dissolving and other more eternal ones become more and more present.

It sounded beautiful, and I could not help but envy her a little. That night we sat on her kitchen floor, sharing with her family a simple meal of bread and curry while she told me her story. I felt so inspired by it that I told her how brave she had been to follow her heart and go and live the life she felt called to live. I knew many people at home who would never have the courage to step away from their known world and venture into such a completely different reality. "The one who throws herself in deep waters shall never ever drown," I remembered having read somewhere, and now finally I understood the meaning for the first time. If she had not done this, she would have truly drowned in a world so far away from the deepest callings of her spirit. Blessed be the ones who dare to follow the longings of their hearts, I thought to myself.

The evening had gone so fast that I did not even notice how dark it had become outside.

I thanked everyone for the good food and company, and Ismael gave me a ride back to my hotel. He convinced me that he wanted to take Yousef and me to the desert on a free trip the following day. I agreed, and he told me to be ready at five the following afternoon to make it in time for sunset.

Chapter 13
Becoming One With the Desert

I spent the following day exploring some more on my own. I visited the ruins of the temple of Amun and stopped by a rounded pond on the way with the name 'Cleopatra's Spring'. It was believed to have been visited by her once when she traveled through Egypt. Since then, the waters of the pool have been considered to have some healing abilities, even though I doubted it. The water was quite dirty, with a scum of algae thriving on the surface. I nevertheless jumped in. It felt wonderfully refreshing. Back at the hotel, Yousef agreed on joining us for the desert tour and promised to bring food and firewood so we could eat and drink something delicious under the night sky. A few hours later, Ismael picked us up in his jeep, and we started driving out of the city and into the surrounding landscape. We passed by glimmering salt lakes, stunning mountains tinted red from soil rich in iron and copper, lush palm jungles, and sand dunes. Our vision took in large areas of date palms and olive trees, areas where locals were experimenting with growing the desert by bringing in cow manure and better soil. They managed to grow anything from watermelons to large sugarcane. The landscapes were truly stunning, and the air felt cleaner than anywhere else I could remember. The dryness of the climate created a perfect environment for healing.

The desert is so different from anywhere else I had ever been: the pale, hazy colors, the vast and open landscapes and empty spaces. Here I could really meet Mother Earth in all her nudity, and if I dared, perhaps I could meet my own nudity, being stripped away from all the trappings of civilization that usually lent me my identity. I felt as if I would eventually become nobody out here, empty and full inside at the same time, just like nature herself. And the more time I spent in that vast, empty fullness of landscapes, the less my busy mind and city thought patterns found support. My mind became more like the vast vistas of nature opening to infinity all around.

After a while, I realized that all my problems and things I used to worry about were nothing but tiny grains of sand in this immense weaving of creation. Slowly, I began feeling as if I were becoming one with the wind blowing through my hair, the same formless wind sculpting the rock formations in the mountains. I began to dissolve my entire personal history into the larger history of evolution and infinity itself, just as Samantha told me had happened with her. The desert was truly a space for losing my limited self entirely.

If I resisted surrendering myself to the landscape and continued desperately clinging to my identity, I might go crazy and never come out again. These thoughts rippled in a little shiver going down my spine, and I hoped it would not happen to me. Or maybe the opposite, that when I let go of myself, I would fully become myself. So far, life had always appeared to me in paradoxes, whose aporias, like the desert, do not support thought.

We traversed dunes after dunes, with no roads or way marks to counter the wind's ability to transport sand in diaphanous veils eventually erasing all tracks the jeep's wheels left behind. I felt somehow strange and liberated at the same time as we left not a single mark behind us.

What if we never found our way back? We had been driving

for what seemed an eternity. Thoughts began to steal their way into my mind and distract me from the wonderful state of meditation I had just reached. I tried to push them out again and comfort myself with the knowledge that Ismael was an expert in the desert and had guided multitudes of people safely out and back again. But how could I be sure that they came back?

The mind never stops for a second, not even out here in the desert. I tried to force myself to put my attention back on the colors of the sand, to smell the freshness of the air, and I felt cured again and could relax into the surrounding colors and beauty.

We were going up a hill when the jeep suddenly stopped. We all got out and realized it had gotten swallowed by sand. Ismael explained that the sand there was looser than usual because it had not rained for a long time. The surface had not been hardened at all, and at times it could be difficult to drive through. He smiled and encouraged me not to worry at all. Then he and Yousef got some tools out and started digging the tires free. They placed a stone under each front tire to give them something solid to catch onto, and soon we were back driving through a limitless space with no roads and no rules except those of Mother Nature.

"Such freedom being out here!" I thought. "Who even owns the desert?"

Back home, when you venture into nature, there are always so many limitations. The land is always owned by someone who doesn't want you to enter. Imposing signs warn of private property. Fences make it difficult to trespass. It is difficult to find places of complete freedom like the desert.

How can we even own land? We come here without anything, and when we leave again, we also cannot bring anything. Naked we come and naked we leave. That means that this Earth belongs to itself and that we might be lucky enough to borrow it while being here. That moment, I made a promise to myself that if ever I were to own land somewhere, I would never put up a private property sign. Instead, I would write something like this: 'This Land Belongs to Mother Nature, and I Have Been Fortunate Enough to Borrow It with the Promise of Returning It Back to Her in the Same Condition or Better Than Before. You May Come and Enjoy It Like I Do, or in Similar Ways'.

We drove for about another half an hour until we arrived at a beautiful spot surrounded by mountains, making a little grail in the middle.

"This is where we are going to put up camp for the night,", Ismael informed me from the front seat. The Sun had started to set, and while we were putting up the camp and making a fire in the middle, the temperature began dropping rapidly.

"Even when it is twenty-five degrees during the day, it can easily get down to zero or below at night in these areas," Yousef told me.

I started to feel the cold already. It was invading beneath my thin summer clothing. Maybe it was because the days had been so hot that the contrast made it feel far colder than it actually was. I got my sweater out of the backpack, and Ismael came to give me a camel blanket so thick I hardly managed to wrap it around myself.

I tried to keep it from touching my skin, because the texture was so rough that I was afraid it would leave my skin ripped open. Maybe that is a bit of an exaggeration, but camel hair is not as soft as I had imagined. I moved closer to the fire to get some heat while enjoying the last colors of the setting Sun on the horizon.

I needed to pee from all the water I had been drinking to try to avoid any dehydration from the Sun and the dry desert climate, so I ventured out a little away from camp, behind a pile of sand, when something happened.

I was walking barefoot and the sand was still warm from being heated from the Sun all day, and when I was trudging up the little dune, a strange and strong feeling descended of being a child playing in the warm sand. In a split second, I caught a glimpse of an entirely different life I had spent barefooted in the warm sand. I remembered the countless times before that my feet had sunk into that loose grainy warmth when trying to walk across an expanse of it, and how the heat would burn its way into the surfaces of my soles so that over time, my skin would turn almost into leather.

It all happened in a glimpse but felt like hours. It was the same glimpse into time that had opened in Cairo when looking into the street woman's eyes. Only, this time it was myself I was seeing into, as if there exists a place where all memories are stored that one occasionally gets a view into.

I didn't know how to really make sense of it, or if it was just the result of my own imagination. My mind was full of wonder and thought as I walked back towards the camp.

When I arrived, the light of day was dimming, leaving the light of the stars starting to appear in the heavens. Millions and millions of stars, in all sizes and directions starting to twinkle down from above. How wondrous it was to be out under the heavens with infinite orbs of light illumining the universe. Nowhere to be seen were lights of modern civilization.

That night, I slept deeply under the camel blanket, beside the warmth of the fire and below the most awe-inspiring night sky I had ever witnessed. My last thought before falling asleep was that if the stars are the eyes of the universe, they are all watching down over me right now. I felt safer than ever in the arms of

Mother Nature.

We woke to the first rays of light long before the Sun even started to appear. The fire had gone out, and it was terribly cold. Yousef and Ismael were getting a small fire going again to make a cup of tea and prepare a little breakfast before we started the drive back through the dunes to the "reality" I had so happily left behind me. We drank a warm cup of *luiza*, the Arabic name for lemongrass tea, a traditional drink for centuries because of its lovely and fresh taste and its healing abilities for the stomach and entire body. I added some sugar to try to spark some energy to withstand the cold before sunrise. We all sat around a little. Nobody said anything as we silently watched the first colors of sunrise.

So beautiful and fresh, this place was really a site to come to in order to gain mental clarity and restore lost vitality, I thought to myself. The Sun finally arrived behind the mountain in a savagely orange orb far larger than I had experienced elsewhere. It generously started to warm us.

I sat quietly, trying to take in all of the amazing sensations. There is nothing more comforting than feeling the warm morning sunlight after a cold night. This is what the Earth must feel like every spring after a cold and long winter. This is what death must feel in the face of life, I thought, waxing a little poetic while bathed in all the surrounding beauty.

When the Sun was fully up, we started to break down camp. Ismael insisted on me keeping the camel blanket, and I accepted even though it was a little inconvenient for travel. It could, however, really become useful again some time out here.

I felt completely peaceful and restored within as we drove back toward town, feeling a little sad this night could not last forever. But I knew I had new challenges ahead, and that soon I would be ready to make the last part of my trip out to my father's land and fulfill my highest purpose and reason for my journey here.

I knew that all these experiences of getting to know the country and its people was part of the totality of knowing my father. No matter how much I thought myself independent from my environment, I discovered it is never true. In the end, our entire existence depends upon this interdependence. I knew that all we have become through evolution has been possible because of the interconnection and interdependence between man and nature. That interconnection is a treaty that cannot be broken if we want to continue living here on Earth, and the more I got to know nature, the more I also started to feel that she needed us to recognize her and care for her, to treat her surface or skin with love and care, and to water her with appreciation and honor rather than with pesticides and chemicals.

We stopped at a lake on the way back to go for a morning swim; although *swim* was a bit of a big word because the salt content in the water was as high as that of the Dead Sea, I discovered while floating around on the surface of the water. Flakes and crystals of salt had formed everywhere around the lake, making it appear like the frozen landscape I knew so well from many winters by the lake at home. Ismael told me that all the locals would come here and swim if they had a skin condition such as psoriasis or a rheumatic disorder. The high salt and mineral content clear up those conditions, leaving the swimmers healthy again.

"Some even come all the way from Cairo or further to experience these unique healing abilities," he added, feeling proud of his home and all its wonders. Surely in these parts, magic is woven into every aspect of daily life, I thought, and the locals truly appreciated and loved their land. It was beautiful to experience how proud they were to take me to these places and share such abundant nature with me. They told me that lately, huge tourist busses had started to come to Siwa, with wealthy people from mainly Cairo or Alexandria. They had heard rumors of its beauty. Being uncomfortable with the more primitive lifestyle and housing, they began buying up land and erected luxury hotels, making the Bedouins work for minimal salaries. Slowly, all the lands, which for centuries had belonged to Bedouins, had been bought up by rich people for businesses that were ruining the culture and making the Bedouins slaves on their own land, or often on land that had once been their own. I could see the sadness in their eyes when talking about this. They told me they were quite worried about what the future would do to Siwa, and how it would look as investors kept building modernized resorts and chain shops.

Apparently, a few years ago, a fellow tried to fight this evolution by gathering the people of Siwa and making them revolt by just saying *no*, and taking back their land, their rights, and their traditions. Nothing really happened, however, and the fellow tired of fighting and so just let things be, and lived in peace before it was too late. Later, I learned that the fellow was my father.

From all I had been told about him, I was not at all surprised.

Emerging back up from the water and standing with my feet where the salty lake banks met the desert sand, my eyes caught something strange and unusual. Right in front of me bloomed a small white flower. I looked around for more of them, but could see only this one. It seemed frail on its spindly stem, but the blossom was beautiful and in perfect harmony. I looked at its perfectly formed petals and leaves, its elegant and thin stem, and imagined how it had been striving upward from the desert sand toward the Sun, all alone, not knowing whether it would ever be seen or even survive the constant heat. How brave was this little flower and how much we could learn from it, I thought to myself. To come here all alone, probably from a seed that had been traveling from far away, to eventually land right here and choose this very dry and harsh place to be its home: maybe because in all its struggle to survive, it had become strong and resilient enough to grow in any conditions. I felt this little flower was a symbol for always fighting for life, for the light, regardless of anyone noticing what we do and how bright we shine. I took in the vision of this little flower and witnessed all its beauty. Now it did not have to feel alone any more. I asked Ismael and Yousef if they knew this flower and if it usually grew in the desert, but they both shook their heads and told me they had never seem one anywhere.

We climbed in the jeep and started driving back toward the city. Just before we reached Shali, for the first time, I gathered enough courage to ask if they had known a man called Ammar, and Yousef instantly answered.

"Ammar, doctor Ammar? Sure, we know him. Everyone here knows him!" Ismael exclaimed.

Apparently, Ismael used to work for him and had taken people who were staying at his place out on desert tours just like the one we were just returning from.

"Before he died, he ran a camp called Salmadari, about an hour's drive from here, out at the last lake," he explained.

Perhaps Ammar had named Salmadari after my mother, Selma, I thought, or maybe simply because Salma means peace.

"What does *dari* mean?" I asked.

"It's Arabic for home," Ismael answered in his strange

sounding English. Peaceful home or Selma-home. Both names were lovely regardless of their meaning or origin, I thought.

"Why do you ask about him? Do you know him?" Yousef asked.

"No, I don't, but he is my father."

Ismael, who was driving the car, almost drove off the road.

"But Ammar did not have children," said Yousef.

"Yes, he does. He simply just didn't know I existed, and I wasn't old enough to search for him before it was too late."

They both told me they were sorry I had never known my father. They said he was a great man, with a slightly difficult destiny. Ismael said he had worked for him and the tourists out at Salmadari. They told me about the place, and how his land was now run by a friend of his called Abdulla, who carried further the vision of the retreat after my father passed. They told me about my father's death. About how he had been found in the desert not far from his land, most likely taken by the Sun and aridity. He was found with a peaceful look on his face, as if he had intended to leave at that very moment. They told me further that the Bedouins had a tradition. When they knew their time here on Earth had come to an end, they would walk out into the desert in the midday Sun without any clothing. Within a few hours the Sun would have carried them to the beyond, without too much pain or suffering.

Mercifully, the Sun on the naked skin would quickly make them so dehydrated that they would become too tired and disoriented to continue, and simply fall asleep in the warm sand somewhere. Enveloped in solar warmth, death would soon follow peacefully.

"Quite a good way to leave, if that's what you want," Ismael commented from behind the wheel.

"But your father might have also suffered a heart attack or something else. We don't know. The fact is that he is not among us any more. Oh, well actually, you look a little like him," said Yousef, "especially your brown eyes, your straight figure, and something around your mouth, as well."

My mother had told me at least a hundred times that I looked like him, so it didn't come as shock for me to hear them say it.

"I can take you out there tomorrow if you like," Ismael said. "I'm sure you are curious to see and know the place. Abdulla and his staff will surely welcome you and take good care of you."

We agreed to go, feeling that now there was no way back and that everything suddenly had become so real. But I had to be brave like that flower and try to shine from within myself in every given circumstance.

Back at the hotel, I paid both Ismael and Yousef for having taken me on the wonderful trip. When Ismael insisted that the outing had been at his invitation, I forced him to take the money and buy some good food for Samantha so she could cook something nice for the whole family.

Chapter 14
A Paradise on Earth

The next day we drove for almost two hours, passing small villages where children were playing in the streets and men sat around smoking and talking. Only a few grocery shops presented themselves along the entire stretch of date and olive groves owned and cultivated by the people. Their main crop and income in all of Siwa is by far dates, which every year they export. In fact, Siwa dates are believed to be among the very best in the world: large, juicy, and with a sweetness from the constant sunshine like nowhere else. I had already eaten quite a few from Yousef's garden, but my stomach seemed to make a bit of noise if I ate too many, so I had to control myself. I had already decided to pick a lot and bring them home to all of my family and friends.

We turned onto a small, sandy desert road trailing off into nowhere, and after several minutes the lake they'd mentioned appeared in all its beauty. I knew we were getting close. I began feeling butterflies in my stomach and tried to talk to calm the butterflies by telling them there was nothing to worry about, that my father wasn't even there, and that maybe the people on the land wouldn't even believe that I was his daughter, and simply think I was coming to try to claim my right over the land, kick them out, and start a business. I didn't know what to expect, but from what Ismael and Nadim had told me about this Abdulla guy, who had been a good friend of my father, I doubted that they would treat me with such disgrace.

We continued along on a narrow road skirting the lake, when we took a left turn away from the lake and continued up a small desert road leading toward sand dunes. A bit further, I spotted various buildings: a few wooden houses and some strangely artistic mud structures. I knew this must be it. The land was enclosed in some natural palm frond fencing, indicating the boundaries.

An inviting wooden gate displayed a large sign saying 'Welcome to Salmadari'. Beneath it, another sign proclaimed 'A New World'. I was not surprised. All the descriptions I'd heard of my father emphasized just how much of an ideologist he'd been, how committed to making this world a better, more just place.

There were no cars parked anywhere, so Ismael surmised that Abdulla and his helpers were probably out. He picked up his phone.

"Hamdulla, Abdulla. Where are you? Yousef and I are here, and we have somebody with us we would like you to meet."

Abdulla told him they were out helping neighbors move goats from one area to another but would be back within the hour. He invited us to just go in, have a look around, and make some tea. This gave me the opportunity to explore a little for myself what kind of place my father had built and lived in.

It was a truly beautiful stretch of land, located on a hilltop with a sandbank sloping straight into the lake. From atop the hill, I could take in the entire area: the lake and the infinite expanse of dunes beyond. Such an extraordinary location I had never seen. I gradually felt something expanding within as my vision took in the vast bleakness of the landscape. The vista invited something within me as expansive as the wide horizon, and beyond.

I began walking from one end of the property to the other, just to get a feeling and an emotional overview over the land. I walked along a little path from a wooden house in the middle of the property and towards the lake, where the path extended out into a raft in the water. A single palm bench awaited there to simply sit on. The bench had definitely been positioned for one to dissolve into the scenery, connect to Mother Earth, and contemplate life.

I could understand why my father had chosen this very site to be his home.

Some of the buildings were unconventionally strange in their architecture, rounded and with no edges. High ceilings reached all the way to the heavens. Engravings telling stories though images of animals and plants invited the imagination. All had been carefully crafted from natural materials, with the shades of color blending in with those of the scenery, complementing and enhancing each other.

Maybe nature needs our help to extend and fulfill her beauty. By creating something such as this, she must feel as if we are truly her children and colleagues in this extraordinary art work of the world. The place surely looked like a playground for humans to explore their creative abilities, and in doing so, to connect with the very nature of creation itself. What better way could there be to reach such connection and unity than this, I thought to myself.

I guess I had never thought too much about how creativity can truly be a path of spiritual development higher than any other. Maybe God is not to be found in either mosques or churches, but rather in the very act of doing exactly what he does. Creating. And in so doing, becoming one with the stream of creation. Creativity is in a way the natural order of life. And life is energy: pure, creative energy. To refuse this truth is to refuse one's self. I thought that maybe soon, it will become common sense that only by creating and moving along with that force of exploration can one truly become one with creation. And only through action and showing up to our lives will we eventually know our true nature and the very nature of life itself.

I thought about my mother and how she had always felt when she was writing. Now I understood the necessity of doing so in order for her to know herself and life. I could almost feel how my father had been exploring himself to the fullest here: able to build anything he wanted in whatever shape and form he wished to give it, with the only limitations being his own mind and imagination.

The entire place was alive with a spirit of creativity and exploration, and I could only imagine how it would have opened up several similar doors within those who visited here.

When I arrived back at the main building, Yousaf welcomed me in a rather Arabic English by saying, "here, tea," while handing me a small cup of this traditional black drink with tons of sugar.

"What do you think?" Ismael asked. "It's very different from anywhere else, right?"

I could only agree while sitting there sipping, still waiting for Muhammad and his people to return. I suddenly felt some sadness passing over me, or maybe it was a wave of deep exhaustion. I couldn't identify where it came from, not anywhere specific. Maybe not even anything from this life. I just felt a deep tiredness and some grief that needed to pass through and dissolve itself into the landscape. Perhaps it was a natural relaxation from having reached my goal, of having arrived at my destination after a whole life of asking questions about my roots.

We waited for at least two hours, and nobody turned up.

Because the exhaustion I was feeling became only more and more severe, I allowed myself to rest my head on a pillow and sleep. "Just for five minutes," was my last thought before my eyes closed.

Two hours later I woke from a deep, dreamless sleep, noticed the Sun had almost disappeared, and that a few men had come back and were sitting around the open fireplace and talking with Ismael and Yousef. I forced my body into an upright position. Then, to my feet. I felt a little insecure, but dragged myself to the fireplace everyone had gathered around. Once they realized I was awake, they all stopped talking and directed their eyes toward me.

"Welcome back," said a man I assumed to be Abdulla.

He looked as if he were in his forties. His beard surrounded his mouth like the shawl wrapped around his shoulders. Strong but slender, he looked more feminine than I had expected.

"It seemed as if you were far away. Where did you go?" he asked.

I told him I had gone to the land hiding behind our dreams, and that the language spoken there was so far from words here that I would only fail if I tried to explain. Actually, though, I remembered nothing at all of my sleep, but the moment I spoke I somehow realized I wanted to impress him. Perhaps it was because he was the one in charge of my father's land. Perhaps I felt that if I did not try to show my best side, he would not believe I was Ammar's daughter. Perhaps he would then refuse me any insight into this place, which could begin to answer my longings to know more of who my father was and of how and where he had lived his life.

Abdulla's skin was darker than most of those gathered around the fire, and even with his body sitting down, I could see he was far taller than the local Bedouins. More African in his look, I concluded, with fuller lips and some almost black curls of hair. Focused solely on Abdulla, I barely noticed the others.

A few young men around my age or slightly younger looked like Bedouins from the area in their shapes and features. An older man with a long grey beard sat a little away from the fire, smoking on a pipe. A woman in her thirties, Egyptian looking, but with her hair liberated and wild around her head, wore a colorful dress and large, golden gypsy earrings. She was beautiful and looked as though she might have been a model at some point.

I sat down on a pillow closest to the fire to try and let the heat loosen me up a little.

"We have told them who you are, Alanna, and why you have come here," Ismael said, looking straight to me as I sat.

Abdulla nodded, sent me a big smile, told me I was more than welcome, and that they were happy to have me here. I started to feel a little more relaxed, as all the stiffness and confusion after the sleep slowly ebbed away.

"How long have you been here?" I asked Abdulla.

"Oh, what a good question!" he replied. "I stopped counting years ago. Time is not so important to me, and even less out here. My age is in the end only a number. I came here as a young lad from down south to work as a waiter in a restaurant, with no experience about anything, and not much knowledge about either myself or this world. But because I always felt different inside, I felt a coherence here with the landscape, and a freedom I had not known from my home in Luxor, in southern Egypt, where I grew up in the middle of the city."

He told me the story of how he was born into a family of ten children, an Egyptian mother, and a Sudanese father. His father had owned a little food stall in the city. It sold Sudanese dishes prepared mainly by his mother, himself, and his siblings. They never had a lot of money, but always enough for daily expenses. Abdulla had even been fortunate enough to attend the local school for a few years. His older siblings had not been able to study because their help was necessary to keep the food shop running. His years at school had been a door into a new world of opportunities and possibilities, and soon he realized that if he wanted to do anything away from the noisy streets of his father's food stall, he would have to learn English and study the world. So, every afternoon after classes, instead of helping his siblings, he hid himself away in a corner of their two-room apartment and practiced all his school work over and over. This resulted in him becoming the best student in the class — even though it was not the grandest achievement. The academic standards, he explained, were poor. Once he finished school, he was supposed to marry and start a family. His family arranged for him to marry a woman from Sudan, from his father's side of the family. He could provide for the family by earning money from working at his father's shop. All had been arranged and planned, and all he had to do was just show up for it.

But Abdulla felt that life had other plans for him, and when he refused to follow Allah as his father wished, they accused him of bringing bad luck and shame to the family. The best thing, they thought, was to get him far away from there and forget that he ever existed. So, his father arranged with a friend of his who had some contacts up here to find some work for him sufficient to provide food and a roof over his head. For two years, he worked as a waiter at a tourist resort. This had been good for him because the guests often spoke English, so it gave him an opportunity to improve his own and to know people from outside Egypt. When working there, he met my father, who was doing photography for the resort.

My father instantly felt that Abdulla was different from most and asked him to come and work for him instead. In exchange, he would teach Abdulla everything he knew about the world. Abdulla agreed. It seemed like the perfect, once-in-a-lifetime opportunity. A week later, he found himself here at Salmadari, this amazing plot of Earth. For more than fifteen years he was a student of my father. He learned to speak English almost to perfection, and also studied history and evolution, biology and medicine, as well as learning to live close to nature, immersed within her magic and her secrets.

"I owe everything I am and know today to your father," he said. "This is why, in return for everything he did for me, I'm trying to continue running the place in his spirit and carry on his vision of the place and his larger vision for humanity. It's not always easy, and sometimes I get tired from the constant work and weight of responsibility your father left me. But it is equally rewarding to live a life of purpose and deep values. The most beautiful tasks in life are also almost always the most difficult ones."

I enjoyed his story thoroughly, and when he asked me about mine, I told him everything: the relationship between my mother and father, how my mother had left him before knowing she was pregnant with me, and how she had brought me up alone, struggling to provide for us because of her health and lack of money. I told him of the bedtime stories she always told me about my father, and the pain she always carried within from being separated from him.

"Your father loved your mother very deeply," Abdulla told me.

I learned that he never mentioned her much. His mind often won over his heart. He had in every possible way tried to erase her existence so that he could move on and not linger too much in the pain. Only the name of this place he had chosen in her honor. It was at least a physical home, instead of the inner home he had once shared with her.

Here, he could live in the arms of Mother Nature rather than in the arms of the woman he loved.

Abdulla told me that my father was far more sensitive than his appearance would indicate, and only a few times in all of the years Abdulla had known him had he told Abdulla about how much struggle and anguish he was often going through inside. Abdulla and he had become best friends and coworkers. My father had slowly given him more and more responsibility, and because my father was becoming older and older, he was happy to hand over some of the weight to someone he trusted and respected.

That night, we sat around the fire until midnight while Muhammad shared all his stories with me of how things had changed here over time. He spoke of how, for a few years, they ran a local school every afternoon for the children of Siwa. They came to learn everything: arts and crafts, language classes, history and science, and how to grow crops in the desert and build your own house from natural materials.

"Those days were the happiest," he told me. "We were able to teach children who would otherwise never get to go to school. We showed them how to do hands-on daily tasks, instructed them in English, and gave them knowledge about the world. The school continued for a few years until, unfortunately, some of the most orthodox Muslim families of Siwa felt as if our teachings here were not in accordance with those of the Koran. So, they took their children out and started spreading rumors about us being anti-Allah. Slowly, no children were allowed to come here any more."

He sighed pensively, and then continued. "Teaching people about freedom is the biggest threat to religion. The more you see and know, the more you start questioning how and why things are being done the way they are. Some of the older boys had been coming here for a few years and had been learning some English along with many other things. All of a sudden, they no longer wanted just to marry a Bedouin woman and work on their father's land. Now they wanted to choose their own way and seek their own fortune in life. And by wanting these things they would often bring shame to their family and their traditions. So, the parents could not risk that such doors would open inside of their children." Again, he paused, and then continued. "You see all these buildings there?" He pointed to one end of the property. "They are workshops built for either woodwork, painting and drawing, or an indoor classroom for study. Tomorrow when it's light, I will show you around the property so you can see for yourself. How long will you stay with us?"

I couldn't answer his questions, so instead I said, "as long as you'll have me."

He smiled and told me that had my father known of my existence, he would have surely wanted me there more than anything in the world.

"He always wanted to have children, your father," he told me, "and often felt sad not to have some of his own to absorb all his knowledge and stories. If he had only known you were here on Earth, I think his life would have been very different. Less inner agony and more joy. But surely, life does not always bring you the relief you are longing for, and often the path is so full of the opposite that one has to remain strong and not surrender to every defeat that comes along with growing up and evolving."

While we sat around the fire, the Egyptian woman with the colorful dress and the golden earrings came and handed us each a bowl of soup and some freshly baked flat bread that smelled subtly smoked from the cooking fire. I had forgotten all about food until now, but suddenly with the warm soup and the smell of fresh bread, I realized I was starving. Since breakfast, I had not eaten anything other than a banana and some dates. After eating, I said goodnight and farewell to Ismael and Yousef, who were heading back to the city. I thanked them for all their help and support, and they told me just to call them if I needed anything.

I sat a little longer, looking into the constant dancing of flames in the fire, contemplating and arranging everything that Abdulla had shared with me. The flames glowed red and orange, giving out the warmth of burning palm branches. Fire is a primordial process, and I remembered one of my mother's friends having once told me that when you burn a piece of wood, it is like burning the Sun. Or that the wood had captivated the sunlight when it was alive and transformed it into carbon, so that wood, when we burn it, is literality like the Sun, transformed. I didn't know if this was true or not but, in a way, it made a lot of sense.

After a while, Abdulla showed me to a hut built out of simple dried palm leaves. It had a bamboo roof with a tarp underneath. It was located a bit away from the main camp, with a view of the lake. He told me this could be mine as soon as I wanted.

Chapter 15
The Mystery of the Desert

The next morning, I had been awake for two hours already when I looked at my watch and realized it was almost seven. I thought I might as well get up, because I was not able to get back to sleep. I began putting on some clothing. Everyone at the camp was still asleep, so I went to find the sandals I had left around the fireplace the night before. I put them on and started walking away from the property and into the open landscape behind the campsite. I walked for a while, not thinking, only walking, one step after another, further and further into the open dunes that extended all the way into Libya. The weather was perfect. A fresh morning breeze filled the air around me with tiny sand corns that made the whole atmosphere seem hazily mystical. The Sun was still coming up in the horizon, and the warmth at this time was far more pleasant than it would be in a few hours. I kept walking further and further into the empty and open landscape. It had a way of reflecting my inner landscape, so I would become empty and calm inside as well. And the emptier and calmer I became, the more I would gladly hand over my thoughts and worries. Slowly, my own personal story faded into insignificance. In the face of these pale, hazy sand worlds, I felt as if I had become one with the desert, when suddenly I saw a man walking toward me.

Strange, I hadn't noticed him before, I thought, for I had been looking quiet attentively at the unfolding landscape toward the dunes. But maybe, I concluded, I had been distracted in thought, as I so often was. As our strides brought us closer to one another, I noticed he walked a little strangely, as if he were limping on one of his legs. His clothing was terribly worn, with his trousers torn at both knees. I squinted my eyes more narrowly to try and see if he was carrying anything, but both his hands were empty. He came closer and then stopped right in front of me, opening his mouth to say something, but uttering nothing. He kept on like that for a while, slowly, as if he wanted to communicate something to me without realizing that his words had no sound to me.

He is just mute, I thought to myself.

He kept moving his mouth without any words emerging. Suddenly, when he noticed the necklace around my neck with the pendant my father had given my mother, he pointed at it and seemed to recognize its meaning. His mouth turned into a smile. Good, a smile communicates in a universal language that doesn't need sound or translation. But what was he doing out here all alone? And where had he come from?

I looked in the direction he had appeared from, but saw no tracks, only soft sand dunes as far as my eyes could reach. The whole situation made me feel deeply confused, and because I couldn't understand what he was trying to tell me, the whole situation didn't really make sense at all.

Then suddenly, he stopped moving his mouth, as if he had said all he had intended. He put his finger in front of his lips and whispered "sssshhhh", as if he had told me the world's secret. A secret I could not tell anyone else.

Then he turned around and started walking in the direction I had come from, still limping on his one leg.

I felt disoriented and didn't know what to do. I continued walking further into the direction from where he had just appeared, and shortly after, turned my head around to see where he was going. To my surprise, I realized he was nowhere to be seen. My eyes searched every possible direction, and still, I couldn't spot him anywhere.

It couldn't make sense at all. As on an ocean, there is nowhere to hide in a desert. Everything will eventually be revealed, even our deepest secrets, everything we carry secretly will eventually surface.

I stood looking, searching. He had simply vanished, leaving no trace.

I felt uncomfortable inside. All of a sudden, I didn't feel like going any further into the desert. I turned around and began walking back.

When I reached the camp, the others were awake and sitting on pillows around the embers remaining from the night before. Abdulla looked at me and could clearly see that something had happened.

"Where have you been?" he asked. "We thought you were still sleeping safe and sound in your bed. Come. Make coffee with me in the kitchen."

I told Abdulla about what I had just experienced.

"Hmm," he said. "I've heard people talk about having had similar experiences. What did he look like?"

I described him. Short, dark skin, brown eyes. He was wearing some strange, very old brown clothing, not like kaftans, the long, Egyptian one-piece shirts the Bedouins wear.

Abdulla remained quiet for a long time and looked thoughtful while concentrating on making the coffee.

"The desert has a way of dissolving time and space," he said after a while. "People often go into the desert to experience infinity. No beginning, no end. The colors and the uniformity of the environment somehow lead you straight into other realities. I cannot explain how, but I know the desert can be a mystical place. It doesn't always abide by the natural laws you find elsewhere. The person you just described sounds exactly like what the ancestors here look like. They were shorter than us, lived in caves in the mountains, and their clothing was brown and rough, woven from palm fibers. I think the person you met out there is not from our time," he concluded.

"But what did he try to communicate to me, and why couldn't I hear him?" I asked.

"That, I cannot answer you," Abdulla replied. "But sometimes the experience is the message itself. What you just experienced is rare. Be proud and don't tell it to many. They will not believe you, but rather think your senses were betraying you. Don't try too much to make sense of it, because it will only make your mind seek conclusions that you might not be ready to accept yet. Just let it abide inside as it was, as it happened, and maybe one day you'll live your way into understanding it more."

I accepted his advice and felt more settled, but then suddenly realized I was tired from the walk and lack of sleep. I went into my room to try to sleep again for a few hours more before meeting the new day and seeing more of this place.

Chapter 16
Everybody Has Their Own Story

I stayed on for a few months. Autumn turned to winter. The days were still lovely and sunny, with cold breezes from the north. Nights grew increasingly cold. Even under several camel blankets, I awoke to a frozen nose awaiting the Sun's redemptive heat and nameless brilliance.

At times, deceivingly innocent breezes would build into wild sandstorms so strong one could not see a meter ahead, and the whole landscape would succumb to a thick layer of sand. Those days were heavy, and we all worked ceaselessly to uncover the suddenly subterranean world of our camp from the underworld and restore it once again to the world of light.

I remembered my mother's stories about the wind, and for the first time felt the power it truly possessed. The desert provided no path of escape. Sand made its way through everything and entered in everywhere. My hut was not insulated enough for those sandstorms, so I would have to take refuge in one of the workshop buildings. Even in that hiding place, the sand would find its way through, leaving a thin layer of dust on everything and a hazy atmosphere. We would all gather around a little stove in the kitchen of the main building, telling each other stories while waiting for the worst winds to pass so we could continue our work outside.

One of those days during the sand storms, I got to speak with the Egyptian woman who had worn the colorful, almost celebratory dress and the golden earrings on my day of arrival. Before that, we had only greeted each other. She did her thing, and I mine. She didn't seem to be a woman of many words, and I could hardly remember having ever heard her engage in long conversation with anyone about anything.

She had been there for almost a year, Abdulla once told me. She was mainly in charge of the kitchen, where she was doing a wonderful job. Her grandmother had taught her the art of cooking, and it seemed like the easiest thing in this world for her. Much easier than talking or socializing.

I found her character to be quite contradictory, paradoxical. In appearance, she was a woman of extreme beauty, with capacious brown eyes, high cheekbones, long and healthy-looking curls of hair cascading in waves all the way down the curve of her back, and a tall, slender body. I could imagine her being a supermodel, earning all the money in the world, choosing between any man she ever desired rather than leading a quiet life simply cooking for a few workers out here.

Her character puzzled me, and because she didn't really give me much of a feeling she wanted to talk, I didn't dare to ask her anything about her life or why she had come here. But one day, the wind trapped us inside the same room. Abdulla and the others were out trying to save some newly planted trees from being buried in sand.

I volunteered to help in the kitchen because being around the fire, in a warm and dry place, seemed like the most comfortable possibility I could imagine. Up till now, helping out in the kitchen had never been my task. I only enjoyed what emerged from the kitchen every day when I was hungry after work.

She was a masterful cook. She knew the art of spicing dishes perfectly, neither too piquant nor too bland. She always prepared the perfect amount of food, enough for everybody to get full, with not much left over. This was important because we didn't have much money and resources to work with. She made sure each dish was always ready at the exact time we were accustomed to eating our meals. This all added to a wonderful rhythm for the body and mind. Some structure to just lean into. And it felt wonderful not to have to plan my own life alone all the time and make all the decisions regarding what to do, what to eat, and where to be.

She needed that rhythm more than anybody. But this day, she seemed friendlier and more open. She told me to peel some potatoes and carrots, and while we were working together in the kitchen, she told me her name for the first time, and I realized I had not even known her name up till then.

"My name is Yara."

I started to tell her mine, when she said, "I know what your name is."

Then I dared to ask her where she had come from, and she told me she came from a medium-sized city outside Cairo, along the Nile. She seemed to actually be happy to be asked, so I thought maybe I had been mistaken about her not wanting to talk. I decided to ask one more question.

"How and what brought you here?"

In response, she told me her story. How she had been born into a devoutly Muslim family, and how from the age of six she had only known life under a burka, always at home with her mother and smaller siblings, either cooking or watching television. She would have liked to go to school, but her father thought it completely unnecessary for her to know anything but how to cook and be a good wife.

As she grew older, she grew more and more beautiful. Her father, who had always been rather poor, was aware of her beauty as a way out of poverty. He was waiting for a rich man to come along and marry her in hopes she could bring some fortune to the family. Everybody in the family and in her city knew about her beauty, even though few had actually seen her face outside of all the fabric hiding it.

No man was ever good enough for her, according to her father. But because the rumors of her beauty had spread as wide as the desert itself, one day, just as her father predicted, a rich man from Cairo showed up and asked for her hand. Her father was overly pleased, thanked Allah, and instantly consented, although he knew little about the man or how he was living.

The most opulent wedding anyone had ever imagined was arranged, and she wore the most beautiful white dress. He, who was a modern man, insisted on her showing off her beautiful face to everyone, because it would be such a waste to just hide it away.

Because she had been brought up to follow every word and demand from a man, she simply obeyed and showed her face in public for the first time since she was six years old. Only her closest family were there at the wedding, for the majority of guests that day were wealthy people from the city, just like her new husband. Everything was a completely new world for her. Alcohol, music, and a table full of any dish she could ever think of. The food was so different from anything she had known up till that day. Her father felt so blessed seeing all the wealth that he was not really bothered about her showing her face to everyone.

"This is modern life, my girl. Here, you'll never need anything," he said with a plate so full of food that he would never be able to fit it all into his stomach. But that was surely not important to him. He was out of the poverty he had felt all of his life, and his daughter would never suffer the same destiny he had. Her wedding had really been something, and by the end of the night, when all the visitors had left, her father drove her to a luxury apartment on the tenth floor, overlooking the city from a rooftop with a jacuzzi and an outside bar area.

Then she was alone with her husband for the first time since they met, before the kind and generous man changed into someone less gentle and more demanding.

He told her to take off all of her clothing. And before he took her to bed with him, he carefully examined and analyzed her body and told her that together, they would be making a lot of money. She obeyed him and got fully undressed in front of him. She did not understand until later what he had meant about making money.

Since their wedding day, he never really spoke much to her or showed interest except for her looks. And because he had come to see and realize her beauty more and more, he felt it was a waste not to show to others. Also, there was the money her beauty could bring him. So, he arranged for her to start modeling.

Within a short while, she was on posters and in commercials all over town: everything from underwear, to toothpaste commercials, and real estate developments. She had no other choice but to go along with it, and if she refused him, her home life would turn to hell. Every day her life grew more and more miserable.

Her family, who was of course surprised about her sudden fame, felt a bit worried about what Allah would say about all this. Still, they were pleased she had succeeded and that neither one of them would ever need anything again. Leaving him would never be an option because it would bring shame to the family and spoil their reputation.

So, all of this continued until one day she met my cousin, Nadim, when she was doing some modeling for some of his products. He noticed in her eyes that something was wrong, and when her husband was out working one day, he pulled her aside and asked why she looked so unhappy. She broke down and told him everything.

Shortly afterward, he helped her to arrange her escape to a place where nobody would think to look for her and she could feel safely exiled from her husband. Nadim knew that a man like her husband would never stop or let go of her unless she disappeared entirely from the surface of the Earth, and Nadim told her he knew of the perfect place.

"This is how I came here one year ago, feeling like nothing or nobody," she said. "Rather broken by all that life had put me through, I was pleased when Abdulla and his people took good care of me and just let me be and do nothing for a while, until I slowly, by the help of the desert and the beauty here, began putting all these things behind me and taking up the task of cooking as a part of my healing." She looked deep into my eyes as she continued.

"My beauty in this life has in a way been my biggest curse. You see, so often I wished for nothing but to be ugly so that everybody would just let me be at peace. But over time, I came to feel even more sorry for my husband. I think he could have been a good man inside, but he had been infused with capitalism and money from the first day of his life, so he was unable to find value in anything else. He thought all the money he was making would bring him freedom. But in a way, no punishment is bigger than being poor in spirit. It's quite contradictory when you think about how the majority of all the women in the world are constantly striving for outer beauty and imagine that by achieving it, they can become free. Well, in my case, it was just the opposite," she added.

"Did you know that the most popular cosmetic products here are whitening creams, and that in Western countries they are self-tanning products?"

We couldn't help but laugh at the absurdities of a fact so tragic and comic at the same time. Why not instead honor our own genetics and uniqueness?

After this, neither of us said anything for a while. In a way, there was nothing to say. Maybe this is why she didn't seem to talk a lot, because she simply felt there was nothing really to say about anything any more. After this day, Yara and I were somehow friends. We still didn't talk much, but sometimes there would be a little smile or some exchange of a gesture between us.

A few other people came from outside to join in our daily life. Some had been lasting friends of my father and others were sick and hoping to cure themselves, especially those sensitive to radiation. They came because they had nowhere else to go. Here, there was no other signal than the light from the stars and the radiating power from the moon at night. These people had been completely exiled from the rest of the world and forced to leave everything just in order to escape what was causing them so much illness. Soon, though, telephone signal masts would also appear everywhere in the desert. The Bedouins wanted to become modernized just like the rest of the world, and where would these people go then? I was sure there would be a drastic increase in people unable to tolerate the increasing electromagnetic pollution: constant microwaves, electricidal fields, and radiation. And with this new 5G? I wondered how the bees and animals could escape. I knew of significant evidence of how insect and other animal populations drastically decrease in electromagnetic environments. Bees become confused and lose their sense of navigation. What would we do when they stop fertilizing our food? And what about our cells? Don't they also get confused and forget what they are meant to do, and instead begin multiplying in one area. All the radiation inspired by capitalism just multiplies and multiplies until the whole body becomes one big cancerous tumor. People will die without even knowing why.

I thought of how sad it was to think about these things, and the high price both we and nature must pay to make this world grow more and more quickly and efficiently, always choosing quantity over quality. Do we even think about the future, about what will happen when we have used up all our resources and there remains only a few animals and insects? If we cannot eat our 5G networks, what can we do? Not to mention, what would happen to the inner landscapes of the people living in a world as such?

I had to stop myself, because all those thoughts made me feel hopeless and powerless. Such feelings often paralyze and make it impossible to do anything at all. Hopefully more and more people will wake up and start claiming back their connection to the Earth by getting together in communities around the world, growing their own food, and honoring the land in all of its glory. I knew it was already happening in many places and that change had a way of spreading like rings in water.

Chapter 17
Music As Medicine

I learned so much from the people and from the land. I helped build a new house, covering the outside walls with a mixture of mud and sand. The Egyptian woman taught me how to cook all her traditional dishes on a small fire. I learned to carve wood and take care of trees and other plants around the property. It felt good to contribute and learn these simple handicrafts, to help with anything as essential as building a shelter or growing our own food. Of course, I had seen my grandfather grow a lot of food when I was a child, but the natural laws in the desert were completely different than those in the wet and cold of my homeland. Sand, not soil, constant sunlight, with rarely any rain, means that nothing grows by accident. All had to be planted and watered carefully. Daily care and attention were necessary, and only by doing so would we be rewarded with vegetables, fruit, and flowers. This is again how we become co-creators of nature. I started to believe more and more in doing so.

We were almost self-sufficient in food from the land. The few things we couldn't grow, we would exchange with some of our neighbors or with the grocers in town. Staples such as flour for making bread, and sugar for tea, we had to get elsewhere. We managed to grow most of our vegetables. However, because we had so much produce, we could sell much of it and make a small profit to keep the place running. None of the people living on the land were either paying or getting paid for their work. Our work we exchanged for shelter and food. Indeed, it was a very simple way of living here, but also a lot of hard work, and I could imagine my father would have grown tired of it with age catching up to him, his life force not being what it had been back in the days he had overcome malaria.

The days were passing quickly, and every day soon turned into a week and a week into a month. One day, waking up on Christmas morning, my little simple palm hut felt almost like the stable where Jesus was born on that holy night over two-thousand years ago. I felt a primitive sense of luxury. I spent most of the day alone, reading a book under an olive tree. That night, we all gathered around the fire for food and warmth. A lot of people arrived from outside to join us, and some brought drums and played a concert that had felt so hypnotizing that I forgot everything.

The drummers took me on a journey all the way from their ancestors until today, telling stories through their rhythms of the changing landscapes and their love for these wide-open horizons. For the first time, that night, I felt how music is the universally expressive language all words wish to express. I felt completely taken by the power of the experience, and how deeply its story had touched me. Music is truly the language of the soul and works as medicine against all sorts of inner pains.

Every morning, I had been training my body with Muhammad down by the waterfront. He had learned certain exercises from my father for circulating life forces from within to the outside. We would always start by first greeting and connecting to the Sun, imagining how it brings everything alive, allowing it do the same for us, and looking into it for a few seconds at a time to connect our small vision to the larger one of the Sun that sees everything from above. Then repeating the same a few times, opening our eyes for a about five seconds and taking in the sunlight, then closing them again to avoid any damage to the eyes. Sun gazing is an almost forgotten treatment for any sufferings of body or mind. Abdulla explained it all. It used to be an ancient practice believed to improve vision, immunity, and generally one's overall wellbeing. Some even said that it would energize them so much that they didn't need to eat as much when doing it regularly. Some didn't need to eat at all for long periods of time.

I remembered my mother once having read a book about a man who had not eaten for several years. Back then, I suspected, the man went silently to the fridge in the middle of the night, because I could not believe that anyone could survive without food. If everyone could live on sunlight alone, why were so many children starving and dying from hunger, especially in Africa, where they have the most exposure to sunlight of all places?

I did not really believe in it back then, but now, after having done it daily for all my time here, I started to feel it did have some effect on my whole being. The movements Abdulla had me doing every morning were gentle and harmonic. Like a dance, but creating the rhythm rather than allowing oneself to be led by it. The movements were created and developed in relation to the stars and planets, and by doing them, one would become more in contact with these forces, Abdulla explained.

"I believe these movement were the very key to your father's good health. He did them every morning before work or breakfast. As you know, he kept himself very healthy and vital until the end. Peoples all throughout history have danced and moved along with the stars and under the moonlight to gain certain energies, but many of these traditions have long been forgotten or not recognized as anything but superstition. Hopefully one day these things will again become prescriptions from a doctor's office, instead of chemical pills, and schools will once again teach the movements to their students, along with the sciences that acknowledge and prove their healing benefits." It sounded lovely. What he told me planted a little seed of hope for a better and more beautiful world; one where science and spirituality start realizing that they are not that separate, that this duality is only an illusion of the mind, that everything is completely interconnected as we see it when we look to nature, and that all matter is also spirit, and all spirit, matter. Sometimes, though, we first have to separate things so that we can understand their nature. The larger picture is simply too difficult to contemplate, but once we have done that, we again need to apply it back in relation to the world. Only then do we fully understand it.

The few months I lived and worked there made me begin to feel familiar with the culture and the secrets of the land. Yet there would still be a lot more to learn. The spectacular scenery of the desert blending in with the fertility of the lakes left a deep impression, all the way into the deepest core of my being, infusing me with magic and wonder.

The desert is alive in such a dignified way. Totally sure of its own being. Dunes might move from one place to another, yet the desert always remains the same. Even though I loved every second of being there, I knew I soon would have to return to my home in the north and continue on another path. There was already so much spirit out here. The desert itself is so magical that everybody surely believes in something higher, or at least in the greatness of the desert itself. And by looking closely enough, one soon realizes there is such order in everything. Nothing seems to be a coincidence. So why wouldn't the same order and laws apply to us and our lives? In the West, it is more difficult. People have long forgotten their origin and connection with this wise universe. They often feel themselves as separate entities moving in a fractured world of separation.

How do we heal this separation, I asked myself. Even though

I generally believed this separation serves a purpose for individuals to truly meet and know themselves, I also believed that we soon would have to start looking for a way back into connection again to save this planet and make it even more extraordinary. I imagined how far we could get if we started working together. Humans and nature. Then there would be no limits to what paradise could blossom on this globe.

I did not know what my part in that would be yet, but I knew I would try everything in my power to serve those changes and make this world more of what it actually could be. I felt my time in history surely was faced with a larger challenge, like any other time in history.

Out in the desert, my mind gained a clarity bringing me closer to my own true nature. I began feeling a strength in my own being I had not known before. I only wished others could have similar rich experiences that bring them to the Center that is both their own, and the world's.

One day, Abdulla told me there was something he wanted to show me, and we walked together to a small little building at the entrance of the property. I had seen the building countless times, but maybe because the structure was cement and square like any building anywhere else, until now I had not even bothered to think about what was inside.

"This used to be your father's workshop," he said. "He built it when he first arrived here so that he would have somewhere to store his things and tools. His things and belongings are still inside, and I thought that maybe you would want to have a look."

I opened the door and saw all sorts of things stuffed into one room.

"Sorry, I forgot to warn you," Abdulla apologized. "Your father was a collector. He loved to make and repair old things, so he would always keep anything he came across. And I think there are some interesting things, like photos and computers full of notes and writings that he created before he passed away."

"It smells like one of those second-hand halls in Denmark that I've haunted for much of my life," I said. "You see, we didn't always have the money to buy new things. Later it become more of a principle from my mother's side. There are enough things and clothing in the world for everyone, for at least a hundred years, we just have to stop throwing everything away after using it a few times and instead buy used things instead of new ones, my mother told me so often I couldn't keep count. This is why almost all the clothing I ever owned was either passed on to me by someone we knew, or bought at the local secondhand shop. For a few years when I was a teenager, I refused to wear anything worn, and to my mother's greatest horror, started shopping in the malls with my girlfriends and using up all my pocket money on a shirt I would get sick of after wearing it three times. But that passed by itself, and I now feel happy again to go to the local recycling and find treasures others have considered to be trash. Even most of the outfit I am wearing right now came from those places, maybe except for my underwear and the shawl I bought in Cairo to wrap around my shoulders."

I made my way into the room and started to orientate myself a little. Furniture occupied one corner, some looking quite handmade, and with strange functions I had never imagined. I guessed my father had been quite an inventor and loved to make things nobody had ever seen. In another corner were heaped piles and piles of books. Mostly history, anthropology, biology, and chemistry. I took a few that looked interesting and thought I might have some time in the afternoons after finishing work to read a little in them. I went into one corner of the room, which was full of electrical devices and old screens. There was a collection of old cameras and lenses from his photography career, along with a few old computers and an endless pile of cables and chargers. I picked up a few hard discs from a dusty box of CDs and DVDs and thought that maybe I would find something of interest on them. I knew from Nadim that my father had written a few books on different topics: everything from romantic poetry to evolutionary novels about the history of nature and human beings. I don't think any of them had ever been published or read by many except his family and friends. Maybe I would find them on some of these hard discs, and if they were worth anything, I could try to send them to a few publishers. It's never too late to become known. So many people through history have come here and tried to make changes, but realized the time was not ripe for it, so they died, or some killed themselves simply because they felt their lives were pointless. They had not managed to make the changes they hoped for in the world, so they left without any fame or recognition, only to become world famous later. Friedrich Nietzsche is one example. He died almost unknown, but now his books have sold second most after the Bible.

I tried to wipe dust from some of the old computers. I didn't even know if they would still work after all these years, but I decided to take the newest with me into the city and plug it in somewhere. Our only electricity was from a few solar panels, which probably would not be strong enough to charge it.

A few times a week, when we went into town to barter or sell some of our crops in return for tools or flour, we would spend a few hours there connecting with people. I would pay a visit to Yousef and sit in his garden restaurant, enjoy some of his good food, and take advantage of his Wi-Fi to send a few messages home, or give a call to my mother, who always pretended she didn't worry about me at all. But I knew she secretly did.

After a few hours in the city, it would feel like such a relief to come back to the land, to the peace and quiet, to the fresh air and the sublime beauty of the landscape. Why would anyone want to live in the city when they could live out here, I often thought.

I took the books, hard discs, and computer back to my little hut and put them away until a better time. Perhaps that would not be until I was back home again.

The days passed quickly without me even noticing. Time is a strange size. The daily rhythm of work, training, and the occasional visit to the city or a swim in the warm spring or salty lakes all seemed to melt together. I knew it was time for me to soon start thinking about returning to my roots. I felt I had found more on this journey than I ever hoped for, and now was the time for me to continue on other paths.

Leaving all this beauty, though, leaving the land of my father's home and all the people who had actually known him, did not feel easy. I knew the time had come, however, and that other adventures were awaiting me along the road. Also, my mother would be happy to have me back. Even though I would move to my own place somewhere, she would feel more relaxed by knowing I was close by.

A few days later, I booked a flight from Cairo. I called and arranged with Nadim to stay with him and his family the night before, and he promised to take me to the airport. Now I had only to enjoy and take in the most from this place, so that its strength and power would always remain in my inner landscape.

Chapter 18
The Reality of Time

On one of my last days, after spending most of the day in the garden with Abdulla fixing some broken water irrigation system going to the olive trees, I was glad to get off work. The weather had been pleasant, with a few clouds in the sky, a rare thing out here. While we were working that day, Abdulla made a big deal out of teaching me just how important olives are for our health.

"Olives were the very first tree on Earth. They can grow in the most harsh and difficult environment and live over a hundred years. When you eat an olive, you also eat the memory it carries from times so different from now, and the fact that they can survive in such a harsh climate as out here with hardly any water means that they have resilience. They are strong tress. They had to struggle for their lives, and the fruits they bring are the result of that struggle. They will make you strong, like them. Some old saying has it that olive trees were the very first tree on Earth, so when you eat them, you receive that memory from the very beginning of everything."

His story impressed me and made me eat a few unripe olives straight from the tree while working. After we finished work that day, I felt more energized than usual, so I decided to take a walk down along the banks of the lake to take in all my last impressions of the colors of the landscapes and the freshness of the air.

I began walking toward the lake, and with me I had brought

a water bottle and some dried olives, for I now believed them to have magical powers. With clouds occasionally hiding the Sun, the weather was perfect for a little exploration. I had not often left the property since that day I encountered the strange man from the past, but today something was calling me to get out there.

I walked for a while. The lake shone a beautiful turquoise blue, reflecting the sky above, and there whispered a mild breeze rippling frail waves in the water and leaving on the banks an almost soap-like ring of foam.

I walked until I forgot everything except the lake in front of me and the dunes and mountains beyond. What a beautiful piece of Earth, I thought to myself. I wished my mother could have been here and seen all this beauty. She would have truly loved it here. As I walked and gradually dissolved into the landscape, something in the sky suddenly caught my attention, and I looked up.

There shone a strange light. To my surprise, I beheld an opening in the sky, like a gathering and formation of light. I had never seen anything like it. To reclaim my sanity, I tried to look off in another direction, but the light seemed to draw me back, forcing me to gaze further and further into its brilliance, which erased everything else around me. The lake slowly started to disappear, and the dunes in the background were subsumed into the brightness of this strange light. Everything was happening so quickly and with such intensity that I started to feel connected with the mass of light the strange light had transformed everything into. I felt united with, communing with everything. My legs began trembling and felt weak beneath me. But in that moment my body was not important. My body felt only like a vehicle for me to take in this experience. The light became more and more condensed, pure energy flowing into matter, somehow creating a strange portal for me to look through. Was this real, or did my eyes deceive me completely? I tried again to look away, but it was not possible any longer. The light drew me in fully. I had no choice but to surrender. It became stronger and stronger and more and more bright until then, in one glimpse, I beheld myself and my entire being beyond this physical body and all its limitations. I saw exactly who I was, who I would become, and why I had come here. I saw every single life I had ever lived and every life that I would come to live in the future. Everything at once. Every single act I had ever committed and every emotion I had ever felt. I understood that time was nothing I had thought it to be before. In this reality I was experiencing no separation between past, present, and future. No separation between myself and everyone else. Mother Earth is me and I am her and everything here in this physical world is only the last layer of sprit, fully condensed into matter, and behind it awaits a completely other world, through layers and layers of matter, gradually becoming thinner and thinner until dissolving fully into only light and spirit. It was all part of the same fabric of life, like a huge blanket woven of everything that had ever happened and would ever happen.

    I knew now that there was a place where all our experiences are contained and remembered. Everything we have ever said, done, felt, and thought, is a complete reality. All of that is a reality out here, as a huge library of memory. I understood now that time is just like a landscape you pass on a train. Just because you have passed it does not mean it no longer exists. I saw myself from my very first life until now and into every future life, with everything I could potentially be and become. I saw my deepest darkness and everything I had once done to others, some things so dark I didn't know if I would ever heal from them, but in the very same second, I saw my brightest and most shining light, my capacity for love and compassion, and my ability to heal both myself and others. I understood that I was nothing but the very universe getting to know itself, that the whole journey of life is to experience all of what it has to offer, and that one day, after all of this, I would return home and know the place for the first time.

I finally understood the poem Mike had left me after we spent that beautiful night together, and I knew now that he must have known these things as well. He had also been initiated into these insights, and this is why he was living in the way he did, always exploring himself and the world. I saw many lives with me and him. One with me being his mother, another where he was my brother, yet another where he was my best friend, and I finally understood that love was much wider than I had understood before. In this world in front of me, he was both my husband, my lover, my brother, my father, and my best friend. The reason I felt so deeply connected to him after having known him for only a few days was the long history of our past lives together. The depths of how we had made love was only to heal that separation of not having been together for all this time. I knew I would never see him again in this life, but it did not matter. I knew he existed, and that is what mattered the most. I saw the lives of both my mother and father. Everything they had been and would ever become. I even thought I would never get to know my father in this life, yet I felt his entire spirit here so strongly, and that was enough, and more than most people knew about their fathers, even after having known them an entire life.

I felt so lovely to be in this light. All I wanted was to just dissolve myself into it and never return to this reality, but just as I tried to hold on to it, it slowly started to spread out and dilute itself, until there were only a few clouds to see in the sky where I had just before seen all of this.

I felt so heavy. My body was shaking, and I had not even noticed I had sat down.

My knees were hurting from being pressed into the hard sand, and I felt the worst headache of my life. Had this really happened? Had it been real, or rather a vision, or maybe even a dream? Had I fallen asleep out here without noticing?

I looked around me, and everything seemed the same as before. The colors of the lake and the beige sand. A few birds were flying above, and from afar I could hear wild dogs barking. The world seemed unchanged, only I felt like I had just had the most extraordinary experience. Maybe the world always looks the same, from the beginning of our journey to the end, but we are the ones who have changed. And the more we change, the more richly this world presents itself to us.

I tried to stand up. I reached for the water bottle in my bag and drank it all, hoping it would cure my headache. Then I started slowly dragging myself back toward camp, feeling so tired that all I wanted was to sleep for a whole week. When I reached the beginning of the land where the date palms grew, I decided to take a little rest.

I made a blanket of my shawl on the warm sand in the shade of the date palms, and slept for I don't know how long.

"Are you okay. Alanna?"

The next thing I saw was Abdulla's worried face right over mine. His forehead had turned all wrinkly from concern. It didn't suit him, I thought to myself as he looked relieved when I opened my eyes.

"Oh, you really gave me a fright there! Never do that again! What would your father not have said if I had let you die out here?

"Yes, but it's okay," I said. "I just felt tired and needed a little rest."

"Did something happen? he asked, as if he suspected something of what had actually just occurred. But I assured him all had been okay, that I simply felt tired and needed a rest after my walk. He didn't seem to believe me, but respected my answer and my privacy to share only what I wished. He knew that some things in life you have to keep to yourself. Some experiences become vain and less magical when you try to put them into words. And those people you might tell them to will never have really felt and seen what you have. So sometimes it´s best to not try to pollute your most intimate experience with words and explanations.

I assured Abdulla I was perfectly fine, and that all I needed was some water. He passed me his water bottle and helped me to sit up so I could pour it into my mouth and further into my stomach to be absorbed into my whole body. Soon after, we walked back to the camp together without saying anything. Everything had been said already.

Abdulla, when he first arrived, had probably been initiated into a similar experience. He understood that something important had happened to me, that the desert had shown me something about myself that was for me alone to know, and no one else. Not even my mother would I tell it to.

Two days later, I found myself again on the bumpy bus going back to Cairo. With me I carried my father's old computer, two hard discs, a ton of dates and spices, and some embroidered shawls and bags made by local women. The roads had not become any better in my absence, and neither had the bus driver. This time, though, after all that had happened to me, I just let all the bumps and shaking be, without fighting or trying to control anything. Everything and nothing are under control, anyway, I thought to myself as I leaned my face on the window and tried to close my eyes.

Saying goodbye to Abdulla and all the others there, the land and the fresh air, and the sublime landscape, had been difficult. As I sat in the bus, I remembered what the light in the sky had shown me about time. Just because it has passed does not mean it does not exist any more. It is just like the landscapes passing by in front of my eyes. They do not disappear only because I have passed them, and I felt better inside to have gained this insight. Nothing would ever be lost, and whatever joys and pains the future might hold for me, they would only weave a further length of the blanket of my own chosen destiny. All I had seen about the future had been hazier and more unclear than the images from the past, and I knew they were merely potentials. Paths I could choose to follow or decide not to.

As I sat there on the bumpy bus rolling over the dusty open desert roads, I felt freer and more liberated than ever before, clearer from all the fresh desert air, and stronger in my body from all the physical work. Within, I felt so rich from all the experiences. And even though I showed up too late to meet my father in real life, I found much more than I could have ever dreamt of. I was excited to meet and know what the future would hold for me, and with less fear of taking a wrong path, because some ways can only be discovered by getting lost. I thus continued into the unknown future. And for every bump in the road, I became stronger and more prepared to meet the challenges and new horizons in front of me. The Sun was setting over the desert road ahead of me. I closed my eyes and knew that the next time I would wake up, it would be morning in Cairo and Nadim would be there to pick me up. So good to have a family, was my last thought before I was rocked into sleep like a baby by the bumpy road and the purr of the engine.